WHO ON EARTH IS DR. PEPPER?

Edited by Ty Reynolds

the writers' group

Calgary, Alberta, Canada

Published by Script: the writers' group

Copyright © 1993 by the Canadian Broadcasting Corporation and Script Publishing Inc.

Cover design by Ty Reynolds.

Individual questions and answers in this book, first broadcast by CBC Radio stations across Canada and used with permission, have been expanded upon.

The CBC logo is also used with permission.

Manufactured in Canada

9 8 7 6 5 4 3 2 1 93 94 95 96 97 98 99

Canadian Cataloguing in Publication Data

Main entry under title:

   Who on earth is Dr. Pepper?

ISBN 1-896015-00-X

   1. Questions and answers.   I. Reynolds, Ty, 1956–

AG195.W46 1993   031.02   C93-090620-9

Printed in Canada

Where did these questions and answers come from?

The questions in this book were spawned in the enquiring minds of CBC listeners from coast to coast. Radio shows that contributed questions are

The Calgary Eyeopener (Calgary)

Edmonton AM (Edmonton)

The Morning Edition (Regina)

CBO Morning (Ottawa)

Information Morning (Fredericton)

Information Morning (Saint John)

Information Morning (Moncton)

That's A Good Question! (network)

The answers to the questions in this book represent the research of many people who work for CBC Radio across Canada. CBC staff were helped out by hundreds of individuals and organizations who provided the information and expertise necessary to answer these Good Questions. Thanks to everyone who contributed.

Particular thanks are also extended to regular information supply lines at federal, provincial, and municipal government departments and agencies.

Who made this book possible?

A portion of the purchase price of this book is being donated to local charities. The donation of proceeds to charity is only possible due to the contributions of time, supplies, and services by the businesses involved in the production and distribution of this book. We would like to thank

- Coles Bookstores Ltd., SmithBooks, and all the independent booksellers who participated by carrying this book
- Canadian Air Cargo- Canadian Airlines International
- Script: the writers' group inc.
- Greyhound Courier Express

for their kindness and generosity.

Contents

Introduction

There's no question about it!

The GOOD QUESTION has turned out to be GREAT!

Let's call it the GREAT QUESTION!

It has come a long way since its humble beginnings in 1981 as a feature on the CBC radio program *The Calgary Eyeopener*. The creator of the Good Question, producer Val Boser, was unsure of the appeal of this new feature so she slotted it as the first item of the day. 6:15 every morning.

Well, it flourished at that time and it remains the first item on the radio program. The popularity of the feature has spawned the *Good Question Re-cap* which is broadcast later in the morning.

Several CBC morning programs across the country have since adopted and modified the format.

If that wasn't enough, in 1991 *That's A Good Question!* was launched. It's a half-hour radio show on the air from coast to coast and yes to the other coast on CBC radio during the summer season. Michael O'Halloran is the producer. John Spittal (that's me) hosts the program. One of the many Good Questions we have received asked, "Why are you the host of the show?"

Good Question! I personally have answered thousands of Good Questions in the past ten years as a member of the *Calgary Eyeopener* radio program unit.

I can honestly say I have never met a Good Question I didn't like. Ummm, but I can think of one I couldn't answer.

It was two years ago on *That's A Good Question!* A listener from Cantata, Ontario wrote in asking, "Why do Canadians say *Eh*?"

Our crack team of researchers spent over two weeks making hundreds of phone calls to find that answer. We tried linguists and Canadian historians, but no luck. Letters poured in from listeners with their speculations. No, it's not because it sounds like the first letter of the alphabet, and forget the explanation that we say *Eh* because *Huh?* was already taken by the Americans.

I still wake up in the middle of the night asking, "Why do we say *Eh*?"

Oh well. One question that can be answered is, "Will there be a fifth in the popular series of Good Question books?" Yes, there is. And it's good reading . . . *Eh!*

John Spittal
Host of *That's A Good Question!*
CBC Radio

What causes hiccups?

The most common cause of hiccups is air in the stomach. Swallowing air is often the result of eating or drinking too fast—even a long bout of talking can cause you to swallow air.

Once in the stomach, this air pushes the upper wall of the stomach against the large, domed muscle just under the ribs. This domed muscle is called the diaphragm. Normally, the diaphragm contracts to draw air into the lungs, then expands again in a gentle rhythm. When the stomach pushes against it, the diaphragm tightens up and goes into a spasm, contracting in jerks. This action draws air suddenly into the lungs. This is the first part of the hiccup.

The second part takes place in the vocal chords. Vocal chords normally produce sound as we exhale, but they can work when we inhale as well. When the diaphragm suddenly forces air into the lungs, the vocal chords vibrate, creating the characteristic "hic!"

This sound is clipped by the third part of the hiccup. A spastic diaphragm is often a sign of impending vomiting. To protect the lungs from stomach acid that could be on its way up the throat, the epiglottis closes off the windpipe. The lack of air stops the spasm in the diaphragm and it relaxes for a moment.

The cycle then repeats itself.

Most home remedies work by forcing the victim to stop breathing for a moment. This gives the stomach a chance to expel the air. Such remedies include drinking water and receiving a fright.

Pressing gently on the eyeballs is another cure. This action places pressure on the vagus nerve, thereby slowing the heart and calming the stomach.

Why are hot water taps always on the left?

Before the days of modern indoor plumbing, only the rich and privileged could afford the luxury of a hot shower. Water had to be hauled to the house and poured into a raised tank, where it could be heated. Pipes connected the hot water tank to the cold water tank beside it, and valves regulated the flow.

In the royal houses, servants hauled water and plumbers built shower structures. These showers were not common enough to be standardized—every plumber built the royal showers his own way. That is, according

WHY ARE HOT WATER TAPS ALWAYS ON THE LEFT?

to legend, until one day a medieval English king—let's call him Clarence the Clean—reached for the cold water valve on the right and scalded himself in the boiling water that poured out. For this affront to the royal dermis, the plumber was beheaded, and the king decreed that, henceforth, hot water would come out on the left and cold on the right.

That, at least, is the story they tell in pipe-fitting schools.

Royal decrees aside, hot and cold water taps were not standardized until they became widely available early this century. Since most people are right handed, they would likely reach for the tap on the right first, so it is safer for the cold water tap to be on the right. This building standard applies around the world, although there are some countries, such as Australia, where the standard is reversed.

In Canada, homeowners have the right to have their taps reversed, although they must also assume liability for scalding any visiting royalty.

When did the first chain letter appear?

According to the U.S. National Postal Museum, the first chain letter appeared in Denver in April of 1935. The Denver letter asked each person to send a dime to each of five people listed. The letter claimed that the ultimate pay-off would be $1,562.50.

The letter created quite a stir at the time. The post office reportedly received 285,000 letters in one day, and by the end of the month the city had to hire 100 extra clerks and carriers to handle the extra workload.

The Post Office declared the chain to be illegal on the grounds that the instigators were using the mail for gambling. However, they were never charged since they couldn't be identified among the tens of thousands of participants.

Who was awarded the first gold record?

The American recording industry awards a gold record to artists whose recordings of individual songs sell over one million copies, but this was not always the case. (Canadian singles "go gold" after selling 75,000 copies.)

The recording industry has been big business since the 1890s. Authorities disagree over who had the first million-selling record, but there are three main contenders for the title. The first and most widely accepted is Enrico Caruso, with his recording of *Vesti La Guibba*, from the opera *Pagliacci*, recorded in 1902.

Arthur Collins' *The Bear and the Preacher* was released in 1905, and is known to have sold over two million copies. Collins was the leading minstrel dialect, or blackface, singer and comic of the 1900s. Between 1901 and 1920, he had 47 top ten hits as a solo artist, and the duo of Arthur Collins and Byron Harlan had 89. During the period that Collins was a member of the Peerless Quartet, the group had 63 hit records.

The third million-selling artist who may have been first was Len Spencer, with his 1902 recording of *Arkansaw Traveler*. With a 20-year studio career that began in 1891, Spencer was America's first recording star. He also recorded many hit comedy records with Ada Jones.

The first artist awarded anything resembling a gold disc was Marie Hall. She was the first female violinist to become a popular recording artist. In 1905, the Gramophone Company of Britain gave her a charm bracelet made of pearls and seven tiny gold discs representing her seven hit records.

The first artist awarded an actual gold record for a million-selling song was Glen Miller, for his orchestra's recording of *Chattanooga Choo-choo*. The song comes from the film *Sun Valley Serenade*, in which the band co-starred with Olympic gold medal skater Sonja Henie. A representative of RCA Records made the gold record presentation on Miller's radio program on February 10th, 1942. The gold record was an actual pressing on a gold disc.

Chattanooga Choo-choo sold 1,200,000 copies in the ten months following its release and according to the RCA representative, was also the first song in 15 years to sell more than a million copies. Sixty-two songs released during that 15-year period have since sold a million copies, but *Chattanooga Choo-choo* was the song that ended the drought.

Glen Miller's gold record was the beginning of a tradition, but for the next 15 years, record companies gave gold records to their artists on an ad hoc basis. It was not until 1958 that the Recording Industry Association of America audited record company sales and formalized the award.

How did Zzyzx, California get its name?

Zzyzx, pronounced "zy-ziks," is an oasis in the Mojave Desert. A drifting miner and preacher named Curtis "Doc" Springer staked his claim on the land in 1944. The land around the oasis is rich in minerals, so Doc Springer capitalized on the health fad of the time by promoting the benefits of bathing in his spring water.

Doc Springer assured his oasis would be the last word in healthy living by naming it Zzyzx. If nothing else, it would be the last word in the atlas index.

After living at Zzyzx for 30 years, Doc Springer was evicted by the federal government's Bureau of Land Management. According to the government, Springer's claim to the land was not legal, and he was therefore trespassing.

California State University later established its Desert Resources Centre at the Zzyzx oasis, where scientists use the oasis as a base of operations to study desert life and geology.

Was *The Cremation of Sam McGee* based on a real person?

The Cremation of Sam McGee is a poem by Robert W. Service set during the Yukon Gold Rush. The poem tells the story of a southern boy who dies in the cold. As he dies, he makes a final wish that he be cremated so that he can finally feel warm.

The character of Sam McGee was based on a real person, but the events are fiction. The real Sam McGee wasn't from Tennessee, nor was he cremated on a barge on Lake Lamarge. In fact, he came from Ontario and worked as a miner and a road engineer. A bit of a drifter, he made his way to Whitehorse during the gold rush of the 1890s. At the same time, Robert Service worked in a Whitehorse bank. According to one biography, Service simply chose McGee's name at random from the bank ledger. According to McGee family legend, however, Service met McGee at the bank, liked the sound of his name, and asked if he could use it in a poem. Although the details of the character's background are fiction, family members say the poem captures the real McGee.

In any case, it is certain the two did meet eventually. A celebrity after the poem was published, McGee expressed mock indignation at the news of his death and cremation. To get even, McGee gave Service the daredevil ride of his life on a riverboat down the Yukon River.

Sam McGee spent his later years in Montana and southern Alberta, but returned to the Yukon in the 1930s. He was amused to find that his name was still so well known that the locals were selling "his" cremated ashes to tourists.

McGee died of a stroke in 1940 at the Beiseker, Alberta home of one of his children.

Why are the arrangement of numbers on the telephone pad and the calculator different?

People who use adding machines, cash registers, and other similar devices on a regular basis soon learn to punch the keys—without looking—as quickly and automatically as touch typists can type. When they use the phone, however, the rows of numbers on the pad are backwards.

The arrangement of numbers on the adding machine is a matter of tradition. The earliest adding devices arranged the base numbers, 0 through 9, so that the lowest values were at the bottom and the highest values were at the top. This tradition was carried on as mechanical adding machines were invented, and even the modern pocket calculator has the digits arranged from bottom to top.

When the research and development department of AT&T was working on the touch-tone telephone in the late 1950s and early 1960s, it was felt that a numerical arrangement based on normal reading patterns of the general public—left to right and top to bottom—made more sense. At that time, very few people used adding machines, but almost everyone could read.

What the research and development department hadn't counted on was the proliferation of electronic calculators only a few years later. By then, the touch-tone arrangement was established, and bookkeepers who make a lot of phone calls have been cursing it ever since. Meanwhile, hunt-and-peckers can't tell the difference.

Why does Wayne Gretzky wear his hockey jersey tucked up on the right side?

The Great One's fashion statement is a holdover from his peewee hockey days in Brantford, Ontario. Young Gretzky was small for his age—even today he's no Marty McSorley—and his sweater was more than roomy. In fact, it was downright bulky.

Wayne complained to his father that the sweater bunched up every time he tried to shoot, which happened as often then as it does now. The senior Gretzky suggested that Wayne tuck the sweater over his hip to keep it out of the way. The records show that Father knew best.

Wayne Gretzky can now afford to find a sweater that fits, but like many sports figures, he has his rituals. If the trick with the sweater worked before, there is no need to change it.

Why do some backyard birds prefer water baths while others prefer dust baths?

If you have a birdbath in your yard, you may have noticed that some birds frequently drop by for a quick splash in the water. Others ignore the birdbath and continue to kick up dust in the garden soil.

Because flying birds of all species depend on their feathers for insulation and transportation, they spend a great deal of time preening and keeping those feathers in good condition. Both water and dust baths help birds do this, and which type they prefer depends on their natural environment.

Birds have a gland at the base of the tail that produces oil. The bird spreads this oil over its feathers to protect them and to prevent them from drying out. If the build-up of oil becomes too thick or filled with dead skin cells, the bird removes the excess by bathing. Besides controlling the production of oil, bathing also helps to control body parasites.

Bathing in water will flush out excess oil and loose particles. Since water and oil do not mix, a protective layer of oil remains. The dust of a dust bath removes excess oil by absorbing it from the feathers. The oil-laden dust is then rubbed off.

Most common birds will bathe in water or dust, depending on what is available, but where they have a choice, most do have their preferences. Birds that are originally from a wet environment will usually bathe in water. Wrens and other birds from an arid climate are more likely to bathe in dust. Though not likely to appear in your backyard, prairie chickens are especially noted for their elaborate dances in the dust, which are also part of their mating ritual.

WHY DO SOME BACKYARD BIRDS PREFER WATER BATHS
WHILE OTHERS PREFER DUST BATHS?

How many ships were sunk in the St. Lawrence River by German U-boats during the Second World War?

German submarines, or U-boats, were a persistent problem for the Allies throughout the Second World War. Even during the "phoney war" period, a real war was being waged in the Atlantic. British attention focused on the U-boat threat with the sinking of the *Athenia* on the first day of the war.

U-boats had their greatest successes against British and American shipping from Canada in 1940 and 1941. Prior to the American entry into the war, there was a cat-and-mouse game between the U-boats and American merchant and escort ships. While America was ostensibly neutral, there were clashes when these ships were fired upon. American ships were ordered to fire back.

After Pearl Harbor, the Germans attacked American ships in earnest. The U-boats also came much closer to the North American coastline, from Newfoundland to the Caribbean. The submarines were so close that they could be spotted from shore, and with weak coastal defenses, the pickings were easy.

Emboldened by these successes, the U-boats worked their way to the St. Lawrence River. On May 12th, 1942, the Dutch *S.S. Leto* and the British *S.S. Nicoya* were sunk in the mouth of the river. Between that date and October 16th, 1942, two escort craft and 17 more merchant ships were sunk, for a total of 21 ships. The furthest inland sinking was about 275 kilometres east of Quebec City; the most aggressive campaign resulted in the sinking of four ships in one day. None of the suspected two or three U-boats responsible was sunk or captured.

The attacks ceased when the U-boats were recalled for duty elsewhere. American and Canadian defenses were strengthened, and eventually the tide turned in the Battle of the Atlantic. But in September 1942 the decision was made to close the St. Lawrence to foreign shipping, greatly hampering external trade for the duration of the war. *The Naval Service of Canada*, the official history published by the ministry of defense, says that "In light of later events it is evident that Canada, in a sense, was defeated in the St. Lawrence in 1942 . . . the Dominion's external trade continued to suffer from the effects of the depredations of two or three submarines during the summer of 1942."

Are dandelions useful for anything besides dandelion wine?

Before its reputation as a weed in an otherwise perfect lawn was established, the dandelion was considered to be a multi-faceted vegetable.

In ancient times, dandelions were harvested each spring and used to help ward off sickness. Raw or cooked leaves and juice from the root were known to restore victims of what is now known to have been vitamin deficiency.

In some parts of Europe, especially Italy, the weed is used in a wide variety of dishes. The tap root can be peeled and cooked like parsnips, or roasted, ground, and made into dandelion coffee. The top two inches of the root, called the crown, can be eaten raw or added to salads. Raw leaves can be used in recipes calling for lettuce, or they can be cooked as a vegetable like spinach. Flowers can also be served raw as a salad garnish, and are made into dandelion wine.

The best time to pick the leaves is when they are most tender, in the spring before the flower stalks are formed. If picked later than this, they may be bitter. Because of pesticides, dandelions should be washed several times in fresh water before cooking or serving.

What is the Roman numeral for zero?

The word zero comes from the Arabic word *sifr*, which means "no" or "none." The idea that "none" could be a number came from India around 600 AD, spread to Arabia, and then came to Europe in the 12th century. The Maya of Central America also "discovered" zero independently about 300 AD.

In other words, the ancient civilizations of Europe and the Mediterranean did not have a number representing nothing. The Roman numeral system had seven symbols—I, V, X, L, C, D, and M, representing 1, 5, 10, 50, 100, 500, and 1,000 respectively. For example, 2,763 is written MMDCCLXIII. A bar over any of the seven symbols multiplies it by one thousand. This system was commonly used in Europe from Roman times to the 15th century. If you've ever attempted a mathematical calculation with Roman numerals, you can appreciate the widely-held opinion that this system was a hindrance to scientific progress.

While Europeans were fumbling with Roman numerals, Arab mathematicians and astronomers were establishing their mathematical reputation with their Arabic system, which we use today. This system is also called a positional system. With a positional system, we can tell exactly what value the number represents by the position of its symbols. Using the same sample number, 2,763, we can tell by each numeral's position that there are 2 thousands, 7 hundreds, 6 tens, and 3 ones. If the number were 2,703, then the position of the zero tells us there are no tens. A non-positional system such as the Roman cannot show this zero value, making calculations difficult.

Roman numerals are now used in non-mathematical applications where they are clearly understood, such as clock faces; where they will be deliberately confusing, such as copyright dates; and where they are pretentious, such as *Star Trek* movie titles.

Why do the characters on the Thunderbirds TV show use the expression, "F.A.B."?

Thunderbirds was one of several "supermarionation" programs created for British television in the 1960s by Gerry and Sylvia Anderson. Some of those programs include *Fireball XL-5*, *Supercar*, and *Stingray*. *Thunderbirds* was their greatest success, with 32 episodes and two feature films.

The characters were played by 22-inch marionettes, and were even drawn as marionettes for the comic book adaptations. Production values were technically sophisticated for the time, and several of the special effects people went on to such projects as the Superman and James Bond films.

The stories revolved around the 21st century adventures of International Rescue, operated by an American patriarch and his sons. International Rescue ran from a private island, where the luxuriant exterior concealed a high-tech complex of hangars and computers. "Everything F.A.B" was the expression often used as a radio communications sign-off after a successful mission.

One central character was Lady Penelope, a beautiful, hip, and aristocratic secret agent who was chauffeured around in her six-wheeled Rolls Royce, nicknamed FAB 1. Co-creator Sylvia Anderson provided the voice for Lady Penelope.

"F.A.B." is an adaptation of the military term "fab," which is an abbreviation of "fabulous." A successful mission is fab; a very successful mission is super-fab. These terms emerged during the Second World War, but by the 1960s fab had entered the vocabulary of British "mods," and is now more commonly associated with that era, as in the Beatles' nickname, "the Fab Four."

Who was the last person to speak Cornish?

Cornish is a Gaelic language that for centuries was spoken in Cornwall, on the southwestern tip of Wales. Cornish died out by the late 1770s, but there is now a movement for its revival.

Cornish comes from Brythonic, a language widely spoken by the Celts of southern Britain. Germanic invaders known as the Angles and the Saxons drove most of these Celts westward during the 5th and 6th centuries AD. This migration split Brythonic into two languages, Welsh and Cornish. Another group of Celts fled Britain for the continent and settled in Brittany, France. Today about 300,000 of their descendants speak a language similar to Cornish called Breton.

Cornwall remained in Celtic hands until 936 AD and Cornish continued to be spoken in Cornwall for several centuries after that. Meanwhile, the language of the dominant Anglo-Saxons evolved into English and exerted its influence. It is a widely-held belief that the last native speaker of Cornish was a fishwife named Dolly Pentreath. Among her last recorded words were a statement she made to an English historian attempting to study the dying language. They translate to "I will not speak English, you ugly black toad!"

Dolly Pentreath was born in a town called Mousehole, pronounced "mou'-zel," and died in 1777 at the age of 102. She is buried a few miles away in Paul. A monument in her honour was erected by Prince Lucien Bonaparte in 1860.

Many scholars dispute the claim that Dolly or any other individual was the last speaker of Cornish. They argue that a language doesn't die a sudden death, but instead fades away. Others, however, point to native languages in North America where there are documented cases of linguistic groups shrinking to one last person, usually a grandparent whose offspring are absorbed into English-speaking culture.

Cornish experienced a minor revival during the 1920s and received another boost during a nationalist wave in the 1970s. There are now about 150 people who speak fluent Cornish. There is a split between those who favour keeping the original, somewhat confusing spelling of the Cornish vocabulary, and those who advocate changing the spelling to accommodate modern rules. Those who prefer the old ways tend to be native Cornwallians, whereas the pressure to change comes mainly from those with an academic interest in Cornish.

What is the origin of "son of a gun"?

There is a touch of grudging admiration for those bold enough to succeed by not giving into convention. "Son of a gun" is a title often given to such an audacious person.

Today it is not usually used as an expression of contempt, but originally it was used as an insult directed at one's heritage. Like many insults, though, this one was then adopted as a matter of pride. According to *The Sailor's Word-Book*, published in 1865, son of a gun was "an epithet conveying contempt in slight degree, and originally applied to boys born afloat, when women were permitted to accompany their husbands to sea; one admiral declared he literally was thus cradled, under the breast of gun carriage."

Voyages by ship were frequently long and conditions were cramped. The only place where a woman could give birth in relative privacy was under the gun barrels, with a blanket thrown up as a screen. A boy born under such unconventional circumstances was then a son of a gun.

How much does the earth weigh?

Since the earth never stops at weigh scales on its travels through space, geologists have had to calculate the mass of the earth the hard way. Based on earthquake data, they first calculated the specific density of the different parts of the earth—layers from the crust to the core, the oceans, ice, and so on.

With this data, they arrived at the average density of the earth, which is 5.517 grams per cubic centimetre. Multiply that with the average radius of the earth, and the result is the earth's mass. That figure is $5,976 \times 10^{24}$ kilograms. This is a geological figure and does not include the additional weight of all the plants and animals on the planet.

HOW MUCH DOES THE EARTH WEIGH?

Did Salieri really murder Mozart?

There are many theories that speculate on the cause of Wolfgang Amadeus Mozart's death in 1791, including the one presented in *Amadeus*. In that movie, Antonio Salieri, a jealous court composer of lesser talent, does in his rival Mozart by poisoning him.

Although Mozart's condition was never successfully diagnosed, most musicologists now believe he simply had a general breakdown. Mozart was under a great deal of professional pressure because of his work load and travel schedule. He also had money problems after his marriage, and it is suspected he had a poor diet. All of this is believed to have exhausted him physically and emotionally. While he was feverish, he believed he was being poisoned; however, documents of the time show that he didn't suspect Salieri of the deed.

For his part, Salieri recognized Mozart's talent. He may well have found the rivalry irritating, but there is little evidence of murderous intent. For one thing, Salieri took an interest in developing the career of Mozart's son—hardly something a murderer would do.

Interest in Salieri's music has been on the rise since the release of *Amadeus*, demonstrating the show biz adage that there is no such thing as bad publicity.

Another aspect of Mozart's life fraught with menace in the film is the appearance of the ominous stranger who hired the ailing composer to write the *Requiem*. The stranger was an agent for Count Franz von Walsegg, who was looking for a masterwork he could pass off as his own composition. Mozart accepted the assignment because he needed the money, but he died before the work was completed.

Mozart was buried in a pauper's grave, and the body has since disappeared. Some music historians doubt that the skull in the Mozart museum in Salzburg is his.

Why is a cinch so easy?

"It's a cinch" is an American slang expression applied to anything so certain and easy it is almost effortless. It has been in common use since the late 19th century, but its roots are in the early days of the Old West.

The Mexican-style saddle used by cowboys had to be even more securely held in place on the horse than riding saddles. After a cow is roped, the lasso is tied to the horn of the saddle. This places more stresses on the saddle, so an extra belt is wrapped around the girth of the horse. This belt is called the cinch, from the Mexican name *cincha*. The cinch is wide and strong, and can be tightened, or cinched, so that it remains secure.

Once the cinch is in place, its security is a sure thing. Anything that is a sure thing is therefore said to be a cinch.

What is the origin of the political pork barrel?

Pork barreling is the process by which politicians dip into the public purse to fund local projects. In this context, the projects are of greater political than practical value serving as payoffs intended to ingratiate legislators with their constituents.

According to students of both politics and language, the term comes from the slavery states of the southern United States. Slaves were fed salt pork kept in huge barrels. When the barrels were hauled out at mealtime, the slaves queued up for their share. This image of the handout applied to the legislative process was popularized in the 1800s, after the passage of the Rivers and Harbors Bill. This bill paid for local bridges, dams, piers, and highways. Critics called these bills the Pork Barrel Bills, and the use of public money in this manner to buy votes became the Pork Barrel System.

How did hopscotch get its name?

The children's game of hopscotch dates back to at least ancient Rome. In one of his writings the Roman author Pliny describes a game similar to modern hopscotch played by the boys of his day. There are also hopscotch markings scratched into the pavement of the Forum in Rome that are known to be from that time.

The early game represented a labyrinth through which the player must navigate by landing on the right squares. As each round progresses, the player must overcome an increasingly difficult route to reach the end of the path.

After Rome became a Christian state, hopscotch came to represent the progress of the soul from earth to heaven through several intermediate stages. The pagan labyrinth was replaced by a representation of the Cross, which was also the shape of the floor plan for early churches and basilicas. The division of the playing court into seven squares represented the seven levels of heaven. The final level, Paradise, is at the end of the court. On the church floor plan, this level is where the altar is located.

Since Pliny's day, hopscotch has traveled around the world, and there are hundreds of versions of rules and designs for the playing court. In England alone, there are dozens of alternate names for the game, including beds, hob-bed, pally-ully, tray-trip, huckety, scotch-hob, and scotch-hoppers.

Hopscotch, the most common name used in North America, comes from the Old French word *escoche*, which means a cut or scratch. The name of the game, literally, is to hop over the marks scratched into the ground.

How many mysteries on *Unsolved Mysteries* have been solved?

The Burbank company Cosgrove Productions introduced its reality-based television program, *Unsolved Mysteries*, in January 1987. There have been 572 stories told between that time and the end of the program's seventh season in July 1993. In that period, 167, or 29 percent, of the mysteries were solved. In most cases, additional information provided by viewers made this possible.

At 75 percent, the mysteries solved most successfully are those involving amnesia victims. Next are the lost love and family reunion cases at 63 percent. Stories about fugitives of the law generate the greatest amount of publicity for the show—43 percent of these stories have ended with the capture of the fugitive.

The mysteries with the lowest success rate are those where there is no name or face available, as in the case of a murder with no suspects. Also very low on the scale are cases of unexplained death.

Audience participation now plays a larger role in *Unsolved Mysteries* than in the past. The chances that a member of the audience could provide clues to the solution of a mystery also plays a larger role in story selection.

Who wrote the theme music for *Hockey Night In Canada*?

The *Hockey Night In Canada* theme has become a second national anthem for many Canadians, but the song started out as just an overblown jingle.

Composer Dolores Clayman-Morris wrote the music in the 1960s while she was working for a Toronto jingle company called Quartet Productions. The producers of *Hockey Night In Canada* approached the company for a new theme, allowing Clayman-Morris considerable freedom with the sound. There was one restriction of a practical nature, however—there had to be a break for the sponsors' announcement of "Brought to you by . . ."

Clayman-Morris says she didn't follow hockey at the time, but she knew she wanted something that sounded adventurous and gladiatorial. First she worked on the main riff, then the chord progression and the theme.

The composer received a normal lump-sum payment for the first five years that the theme was used. Since the end of that period, she has received royalty payments for every time it is used in a broadcast, and, since 1989, has been named in the closing credits. The theme has also been recorded by a Canadian jazz group called The Shuffle Demons.

What is the origin of the term "tin ear"?

"Tin ear" is a 20th century term with several meanings.

The first meaning comes from the 1920s. A tin ear was a square—a person who didn't appreciate jazz music. Such a person can't tell the difference between good music and bad. The reference to tin comes from the tinny, flat sound of an instrument that is out of tune.

From the jazz clubs to the boxing ring, tin ear then became another term for cauliflower ear. Boxers who suffered numerous injuries to the side of the head often developed thick calloused tissue on the outer ear. An irritating and sometimes disorienting ringing in the ear is also associated with these injuries. The cauliflower ear gets its name from the callous's resemblance to the vegetable.

In current usage, having a tin ear means being unable to distinguish between the frequencies of different musical notes.

What is the purpose of a passenger-side mirror that shows a distorted image?

Many side-view mirrors on cars have the warning "objects are closer than they appear" printed on them. This message is on most cars produced in North America since the early 1980s. Relying on the wide angle image reflected in this mirror can be more of a hazard than a help if not used properly.

According to the Standards and Regulations Department of Transport Canada, the side-view mirror isn't supposed to provide an accurate view of what's behind you—that's what the rear-view mirror is for.

The side-view mirror is designed to provide just that—a side view. This mirror shows the driver what is right beside the vehicle. Adjusted properly, the wide-angle mirror allows the driver to see what is to the right with a minimum of head or eye movement away from the road ahead. If the side-view mirror were made of normal glass, the field of view from such an oblique angle would be very narrow, and there would be a huge blind spot. Curved glass eliminates the blind spot, but the perspective is exaggerated.

Side-view mirrors are required by law only on vehicles that do not have a rear-view mirror that provides a certain field of view. The message that "objects are closer than they appear" is required by American law, but is optional in Canada.

Why are polar bears pigeon-toed?

Pigeon-toed feet of polar bears are hardly the result of poor posture. They are an adaptation that allow them to survive in their environment.

Polar bears are large and heavy-set. They also move quickly compared to other animals of similar structure. For these reasons they need the added balance provided by legs that bow outward and feet that point inward give them.

All species of bears are pigeon-toed. Skeletons of the gigantic prehistoric species of bears show that they were also pigeon-toed. This characteristic is more noticeable with polar bears because they have feet that are proportionately twice the size of other species. The larger feet give them the greater support necessary for walking and running on snow and ice.

WHY ARE POLAR BEARS PIGEON-TOED?

Who wrote the music to *The Star Spangled Banner*?

Francis Scott Key entered the pantheon of American folk heroes when he wrote the lyrics to the song that would eventually become the national anthem of the United States. A lawyer by trade, Key wrote the words in September, 1814 during the British siege of Fort McHenry, near Baltimore.

The story behind the music is somewhat less heroic.

The tune was lifted from the English drinking song, *To Anacreon in Heaven*, written in 1780 by John Stafford Smith. The original lyrics accompanying this tune were written by Ralph Tomlinson, president of the Anacreontic Society of London. Members of the society were amateur musicians who met every two weeks at the Crown and Anchor Tavern for a concert, dinner, and merrymaking. The president of the society opened every meeting by singing this song to the members, who joined in on the refrain.

The song and the society take their names from Anacreon, an ancient Greek poet famous for his devotion to wine, women, and song. In the lyric to the song, the self-proclaimed sons of Anacreon describe a battle among the gods, with Venus and Bacchus triumphant. The song concludes with:

> While thus we agree, our toast let it be,
> May our club flourish happy, united, and free!
> And long may the sons of Anacreon entwine
> The myrtle of Venus with Bacchus's vine.

There had been some debate over the true origin of *The Star Spangled Banner* until 1909, when the government published an exhaustive document entitled *Historical Report on The Star Spangled Banner, Hail Columbia, America, and Yankee Doodle*. What remains unclear is whether Key consciously metered his poem to fit the song, or whether, as some argue, Judge Joseph Hopper Nicholson was the first to combine words and music.

The Star Spangled Banner did not become the official national anthem until 1931, replacing *Hail Columbia*.

Why do sailors drink rum?

Rum and the British navy go back to the days of pirates and privateers in the Caribbean. The first written record of rum issued to sailors is from a ship's log of a trip to Jamaica dated 1655.

At that time, ships were unable to store water or beer for long periods of time without the supplies spoiling. Water was easily contaminated by bacteria, and beer turned sour or stale. Rum, however, lasted much longer than either of these when stored in wooden casks.

Beer remained part of a sailor's rations until 1822, when the Admiralty officially replaced it with rum. The rum rations were part of a marketing ploy—since the Navy no longer "pressed," or forced men into service, the sailor's life had to be made more attractive to potential recruits. The Admiralty set up a business to supply all ships with rum rations. The ration was eliminated in 1970 because modern storage techniques made it unnecessary.

With the rum business gone, the Admiralty went to the British Treasury for compensation to the tune of three million pounds, which was used to establish a sailors' trust fund.

The standard grog ration was two parts water to one part rum, or about 2½ ounces of spirits. The slang word grog comes from the nickname given to Edward Vernon, a British admiral who, in 1740, ordered that all alcohol served to sailors be mixed rather than pure. Vernon was known as Old Grog, the name coming from his cloak, which was made of a coarse fabric called grogram.

What makes cheddar cheese orange?

Cheddar was originally a cheese made in the village of Cheddar, in the English county of Somersetshire. The origin of the cheese is unknown, but the first use of the name for the cheese was recorded in 1666. At that time, the cheese was made from either ewes' milk or skimmed cows' milk.

Cheddar cheese was originally white, and is still produced that way in some parts of the world, including Quebec. The first orange cheddar from Cheddar was coloured with the petals of marigolds. Modern cheddar producers use the natural dye beta carotene to colour the cheese orange. Beta carotene is found in carrots and in the seeds of the annatto, a small Caribbean tree. United Empire Loyalists brought the recipe for cheddar with them to Canada, establishing a hundred-year-old reputation for aged Canadian cheddar that has superseded the original. In fact, Canada's largest market for cheddar cheese is Great Britain.

Why were coins placed on the eyes of the dead before burial?

Coins covered the eyes of the dead for two main reasons. The first was to keep the eyes closed. Most cultures view the death of the body as a form of sleep, as in our culture's expression, "Rest In Peace." This sleep allows the soul to leave the material world for a better place.

Approximately ten percent of human deaths occur with eyes open. In these cases, the body is not seen to be "resting." The eyes are closed before burial so that the soul is not trapped. Modern morticians know enough about the human body to make it look natural, but in earlier times the weight of coins was needed to keep the eyes closed.

The second reason concerns the coins themselves. They are the symbolic payment for passage from this world to the next. Archaeological evidence shows that even in prehistoric times, human beings have buried along with their dead a number of material items for use in the great beyond, including weapons, food, jewellery, and in the case of children, toys. The practice of burying money with the dead dates back to at least ancient Greece.

As a symbolic gesture, placing coins on the eyes of the dead carried on into the Christian world. It lasted well into the 17th century, and is still occasionally practiced in Europe.

According to legend, the coins were used by the soul to pay Charon, the ferryman at the River Styx. Without the fare, the soul was condemned to roam for all eternity.

Does anyone really read the flyer inserts in the newspaper?

It's a safe bet that if businesses continually spend money on a certain practice, the return on that practice justifies the expense. On that basis, newspaper inserts pay their way.

According to a 1990 study by the Newspaper Marketing Bureau, 54 percent of Canadian adults read the inserts from grocery stores. Department store inserts have an even higher readership at 60 percent.

A similar American study from 1988 found that 85 percent of adults read the inserts at least sometimes, and 65 percent said they almost always read them.

These figures compare favourably with readership data on non-advertising portions of the paper. Some surveys have shown regular readership of the editorial page to be as low as four percent.

Did the original discoverers of Klondike gold get rich?

The Klondike Gold Rush started in 1896, and was responsible for the opening of the Canadian northwest. The rush developed in two stages. The first of these began when a Canadian prospector named Bob Henderson tipped off George Washington Carmack that there could be gold in the area. Carmack and his native brothers-in-law, Skookum Jim and Tagish Charley, discovered gold in Rabbit Creek on August 16th. Miners and prospectors in the area immediately staked their claims along every available river and creek bed. Rabbit Creek, a tributary of the Klondike River, was later renamed the more suitable Bonanza Creek.

The second stage began a year later, when a Seattle newspaper reported on the large finds in the north. This touched off a four-year stampede of American gold seekers. Most of the hundred thousand who arrived were amateurs unprepared for the harsh northern conditions. Nevertheless, the town of Dawson soon had a floating population of 30,000, making it the largest city north of Seattle and west of Winnipeg.

Dawson experienced the trappings of a frontier boom town, with saloons, dance halls, gambling, and prostitution, plus electricity, telephones, and movie theatres. Law and order was maintained by the North-West Mounted Police, while a military unit called the Yukon Field Force protected Canada's sovereignty.

American interest in Klondike gold began to wane after the start of the Spanish-American War, and after the discovery of gold in Alaska. Over the initial five-year period of the Klondike rush, prospectors extracted 50 million dollars worth of gold from the Klondike. This is also approximately the same amount of money they spent trying to get there and find it.

George Washington Carmack's find was substantial,

and when he died in 1922, he left behind a wealthy estate. Bob Henderson never found gold, but the federal government recognized the importance of his contribution. For his part in the Klondike discovery, the government awarded Henderson a very comfortable lifetime income of two hundred dollars a month. Henderson died in 1933.

How do film actors make themselves cry on cue?

Learning to cry at the right moment is a skill that stage actors practice mainly through two techniques. The first is for the actor to recall a personal experience that dredges up emotions powerful enough to trigger this response. The second is to concentrate on the character and what he or she is going through. With this method, the actor is able to work with the scene to produce the desired results. Either way, the actor goes through an emotional wringer.

On the stage, the actor plays each scene only once or occasionally two times a day. For a film or television program, the actor may have to play the same scene many times over in a matter of hours. When this happens, the ducts dry up and tears are not enough.

When the actor is unable to produce tears, the make-up person steps in with a menthol tube. Menthol is the strong-smelling alcohol used in cold medicines, mints, and some filtered cigarettes. The menthol tube is about three inches long with a drop of menthol on one end. The make-up person blows the menthol into the actor's eyes, causing them to water as much as before.

There is a way to tell if an actor's tears are genuine. If you can see the tears well up in the course of a single shot, they're the real thing. If the camera shows the distraught character, cuts away to another shot, then cuts back to a crying shot, then the tears are probably induced rather than natural.

Do fish "drink like a fish"?

Freshwater fish don't have a drinking problem. In fact, they don't drink at all. On the other hand, saltwater fish are drinking all the time.

Both types of fish have the same amount of salt in their bodies, but saltwater is saltier. This means that water is drawn out of the saltwater fish by the process of osmosis. The saltwater fish must replace this water by drinking so that it doesn't dehydrate. The average saltwater fish drinks about a cup of water per hour for every two pounds of body weight.

For freshwater fish, this osmosis is reversed. The fish absorbs water through its skin and gills, so it doesn't need to drink.

"Drinking like a fish" is usually applied to drinking alcohol, so what would happen to fish swimming in

DO FISH "DRINK LIKE A FISH"?

booze? A group of university students conducted a series of experiments of dubious scientific validity to find out. The fish suffocated in the carbon dioxide in beer, and the alcohol of every drink poisoned them, and the students as well.

Who was the first licensed pilot?

It wasn't long after the first flight of Wilbur and Orville Wright that somebody thought the practice should be regulated. The *Fédération Aéronautique Internationale* was established in France in 1908 and began issuing licenses the following year.

Many pilots from around the world carried licenses issued by the FAI. In addition, many flying clubs associated with the FAI issued their own licenses.

The Wright brothers were among the earliest licensed flyers, but they were not the first. That honour goes to French pilot Louis Blériot, whose license was issued on January 7, 1909.

Blériot was a leading aviation pioneer in his own "wright." Between 1900 and 1903, he experimented with flapping-wing designs, then with box-kite biplanes and a tail-first monoplane. In 1906, he switched to conventional monoplanes.

On July 25, 1909, he flew a 28-horsepower monoplane, the *Blériot XI*, across the English Channel, from Calais to Dover, in 36.5 minutes. For this he won 1,000 pounds offered by the London *Daily Mail*.

With this success, Blériot established a plant that built some of the most advanced monoplanes of the era. During World War I, his plant produced ten thousand planes for the French Army, including the famous Spad fighter. The plant continued to manufacture military and civilian aircraft until 1935. Blériot died in 1936.

Who on earth is Dr. Pepper?

The soft drink named after the good doctor was developed in the 1880s by Charles Alderton, a pharmacist who worked at the Morrison Drug Store in Waco, Texas.

According to company legend, the story began in Virginia, where Wade Morrison was employed as a pharmacist. While working in the drugstore, he was smitten by his boss's daughter. Unfortunately, his boss didn't care for Morrison as a possible son-in-law, so he terminated the romance. The owner of the Virginia pharmacy was a dentist by the name of Dr. Charles Pepper.

Heartbroken, Morrison moved to Waco and opened his own drug store. A standard feature of drug stores in those days was the soda fountain. Morrison noticed that sales at his fountain were slipping due to customer boredom with the same old fruit-flavoured sodas. To add a little pizzazz to the selection, Morrison's employee Charles Alderton experimented with different fruit flavour combinations until he came up with a blend that satisfied Morrison.

The new drink also satisfied the customers. Morrison still carried a flame for Miss Pepper back in Virginia, so his customers suggested that the new drink be named after her father as a way of getting into his good graces. It didn't work, but at least the drink became so popular that other drug stores and soda fountains in the Waco area were soon buying the Dr Pepper syrup and serving the soft drink to their customers as well.

That's the old company version, anyway. The problem with the love angle is the recent discovery that Dr. Pepper's daughter was a mere child when Alderton invented the soft drink in 1885. The Dr Pepper company now believes that aspect of the story was a romantic fabrication that has been handed down until it was accepted as the truth, and that Morrison simply named the drink, minus the period, out of respect for his old mentor. Relations between Pepper and Morrison seem to be satisfactory now—Dr. Pepper's descendants hold a family reunion every year, with refreshments supplied by his namesake.

Dr Pepper remained a Texas drink until it received national exposure at the St. Louis World Fair in 1904. As for Morrison's Drug Store, it is still standing.

Why do we clink glasses to make a bride and groom kiss?

This is a tradition that is usually exercised during the reception dinner. At a moment when things are getting too quiet, one of the guests taps cutlery against a glass or plate. Soon everyone joins in and the noise continues until the couple kisses.

This is an abbreviated version of a toast. Instead of clinking on the glass to get everyone's attention, then stating the toast, then drinking the toast, then kissing, the process is shortened to its beginning and end.

The roots of this practice are recorded in *The History of the Kings of Britain*, written by Geoffrey of Monmouth in 1137. According to this work, which is also the source of the Arthurian legends, British king Vortigern hosted a banquet for his allies, the Saxons, in 450 AD. Rowena, the Saxon king's beautiful daughter, caught Vortigern's fancy, so to break the ice, he made a toast.

"Lord King, be of good health," he declared. Then he drank to his guest's health, swept Rowena off her feet, and kissed her passionately. But he didn't stop there. Intoxicated with mead and lust, he continued to make love to her, and asked her father for her hand in marriage. They were married that evening.

The tradition was born, with a few alterations. These days you have to get married first.

Why do some people have an innie bellybutton and others have an outie?

The bellybutton is really just a scar. After a baby is born and the umbilical cord is cut, blood stops flowing to the cord. Without this blood, the cord dries up, withers, and eventually drops off.

Meanwhile, the opening in the body where the umbilical cord was connected must be sealed. Skin grows to close the opening, just as skin will grow to seal any open wound. Since the belly wall of children is thin, whether one has an innie or an outie depends on how thick the scar tissue over this hole grows. Thick tissue produces an outie; thinner tissue produces an innie.

The belly wall thickens with age, but remains thin under the bellybutton. As a result, an outie often recedes and becomes an innie as a child grows up.

How fast is the earth moving?

The earth's movement through space can be looked at several ways. The planet rotates on its axis, revolves around the sun, and, as part of the solar system, moves through the galaxy.

The speed of the first motion—the rotation of the earth—depends on the point of reference being used. In other words, even though the spin of the earth is constant, the traveling speed of the surface varies with one's latitude. The earth's rotational speed at the equator is approximately 1200 kilometers per hour, while at the north and south pole, the rotational speed is zero kilometers per hour.

In order to make the trip around the sun in 365 days, the earth is traveling 108,000 kilometers per hour, or 30 kilometers per second. Then, along with the sun and the rest of the solar system, we're moving an additional 370 kilometers per second through the Milky Way.

How did St. Peter get the job of guarding the Pearly Gates?

According to tradition, St. Peter holds the keys to the gates of Heaven. Whether or not one is allowed to cross the threshold depends on what is written under one's name in the Book of Judgment. This perception is so widespread that it transcends strictly religious imagery.

Peter was a fisherman named Simon until he joined Jesus, who changed his name to Peter, meaning "rock." He was one of the more important disciples—there are more stories in the Gospels about him than any of Jesus' other followers. Despite his closeness to Jesus, he was the follower who denied three times that he knew Jesus, even though he was warned he would do so.

After the Crucifixion, Peter became a missionary, as related in the Book of Acts. In 41 AD, he became the Bishop of Rome, making him the first Pope of the Christian Church. Papal authority, and the tradition of St. Peter at the gates, comes straight from the word of Christ himself. In the book of Matthew, He says, "Thou art Peter, and upon this rock I will build my church . . . I will give unto thee the keys of the Kingdom of Heaven, and whosoever thou shalt bind on earth shall be bound in Heaven . . ."

Although the death of Peter is not described in the Bible, legend says he was sentenced by Emperor Nero to death by crucifixion in about 66 AD. At his request, Peter was crucified upside down, since he did not feel he was worthy of the same death as Christ.

The bones buried under the high altar of St. Peter's Cathedral in Rome are said to be those of Peter. Exercising the authority handed down through the centuries, Pope Paul VI confirmed their authenticity in 1968.

Why are the knots in lumber so much harder than the surrounding wood?

The knots in wood are the remainder of the tree's branches. Every year, a tree develops another ring of growth around its circumference, just under the bark. These are the rings we see in a tree stump that allow us to determine its age.

As the tree ages, the new rings grow around existing branches. As the branches grow and develop their own rings, each new layer in the main trunk offers greater support. The pressure from trunk growth is balanced by pressure from growth in the branch. We can see this in cut lumber where the grain of the wood flows around the knot.

When one of these branches dies, breaks off, or is pruned, the new growth of the trunk continues around the dead branch or branch stub. This newest growth also continues to exert pressure on that part of the dead branch imbedded in the trunk. The cells of the dead branch are then compacted by this pressure, making the knot more dense and therefore harder than the surrounding living wood.

This pressure on the knot also forces out moisture, causing the knot to change to its characteristic darker colour.

What's the difference between espresso coffee beans and regular coffee beans?

Regular coffee and espresso are made from the same beans. The difference between them begins at the roasting stage. The longer the beans are roasted, the darker they become. Regular coffee can be light, medium, or dark roast. Espresso is made from the darkest roast.

Once the beans are roasted and ground, espresso is made by forcing steaming hot water through the grounds. It is from this forced steaming that the drink gets its name. The Italian name, *caffe espresso*, means "pressed coffee."

Cappuccino is simply espresso topped with foamed milk; café au lait is strong coffee with an equal amount of hot milk.

WHAT'S THE DIFFERENCE BETWEEN ESPRESSO COFFEE BEANS AND REGULAR COFFEE BEANS?

If a tom cat is male, why is a tom boy female?

For centuries in Britain, Tom has been used as a generic male name, just as Joe is a generic name in the Americanism, "regular joe". Similarly, Sheila is a generic name for any woman in Australia. Tom was so common a name it appears in many English slang phrases, such as tomfool, Tom Farthing, Tom Tiler, Tom Tram, Tom Long, peeping Tom, and Tom O'Bedlam.

Until the mid-1800s, the male of any bird or animal species was called a tom. Tom cat and tom turkey are the only cases of tom being commonly used this way today. Although tom cat accurately applies to any male cat, it is often used to refer specifically to male cats on the night prowl for females, hence the verb tomcatting as applied to men on the prowl for women.

Tom boy also comes from tom as a male name. In the 16th century, a tom boy was a common fellow—a boisterous, rude, and promiscuous young man. Then any unchaste woman was also called a tom boy. Double standards being what they are, she was thought to be acting more like a man than a woman.

By the 17th century, tom boy applied specifically to prostitutes. The name was shortened to Toms, and their clients became known by another generic male name: Johns.

Throughout the late 1800s and early 1900s, tom boy lost its sexual connotation and now more innocently means a spirited young girl who enjoys the same activities as young boys. A memoir written by a female writer published in 1876 says, "Tomboyism is a wholesome delight in rushing about at full speed, playing at active games, climbing trees, rowing boats, making dirt pies, and the like." This image of a tom boy as a girl who can do anything a boy can do was fostered by children's literature of the period, from *Tom Sawyer*'s Becky to the title character of *Anne of Green Gables*.

Where does the expression "rob Peter to pay Paul" come from?

Despite the reference to these two disciples, robbing Peter to pay Paul does not come from the Bible, as is commonly thought. Instead, the expression comes from two cathedrals named after the saints.

St. Peter's Abbey Church was upgraded to a cathedral in December, 1540. Ten years later, St. Peter's Cathedral joined the Diocese of London, where St. Paul's Cathedral was already located.

To help finance repairs to the older St. Paul's Cathedral, many of the estates owned by St. Peter's were appropriated. The expression, which means borrowing money from one creditor to pay down a debt to another, entered the language almost immediately.

Why is the third molar of each jaw called a wisdom tooth?

The molars we call the wisdom teeth are the last to emerge. They usually grow in between the ages of 17 and 25, supposedly the time in a person's life when they learn the ways of the world.

These teeth have been associated with the onset of maturity since at least the time of Hippocrates. The medical name for wisdom teeth is *dentes sapientiae*, which literally means teeth of wisdom. This Latin term was discarded in favour of the English in an anatomy book published in 1668.

Cutting one's wisdom teeth is an expression that means "to reach the years of discretion." The first published use of this phrase meaning intellectual or emotional maturity was in a novel published in 1809.

What is the difference between table salt, rock salt, and sea salt?

Each of these salts are all the same chemical compound, sodium chloride. The differences between them lies in their purity.

Table salt is the purest. Its purity of 99.96 percent is achieved by evaporating it through a device called a vacuum pan. Table salt also contains iodine as a means of protecting the public against goitre, a disease of the thyroid gland. Iodine was first added to table salt in the 1940s.

Rock salt is used in many communities to melt ice on roads and sidewalks. It also causes cars to rust prematurely. This salt is mined, and has a purity of about 96 to 98 percent. Since it is not intended for consumption, its purity is not guaranteed. For those who prefer a coarser salt, pickling salt, which has the same purity as table salt, is recommended.

Sea salt, also known as solar salt, has become fashionable among those in faddish health food circles because of its reputation of being more natural. Packaged sea salt comes from ocean water that is poured into open pits and evaporated in the sun. This salt is not as pure as table salt.

How do whales and dolphins sleep under water?

Sea mammals don't sleep for extended periods like land animals, nor do they experience the same type of sleep.

When the time comes for a whale or dolphin to hit the hay—or the seaweed—it doesn't slip into total unconsciousness. Instead, it remains aware of its surroundings and is able to float just beneath the surface of the water. Dolphins are also able to slow down their metabolism while in this state so they are able to remain under water longer than normal.

Both whales and dolphins are able to sleep under water for up to two hours. When it is time for a fresh breath, an automatic reflex is triggered allowing them to drift to the surface, expel the old air, and breathe in fresh oxygen. These breathing characteristics are also shared by other sea mammals, such as seals.

While sleeping in a semi-conscious state, sea mammals are usually able to avoid other objects in the water. Collisions with ships are rare, but when they do occur, it is usually a sperm whale that was caught napping.

Why do a donkey and an elephant represent the Democratic and Republican parties?

The donkey was first associated with the Democrats in 1828. During the election campaign of that year, opponents of Andrew Jackson referred to him as a jackass. Instead of fighting off the insults, Jackson adopted the hard-working donkey as the party's symbol. The maneuver must have worked—Jackson was elected for two terms.

Cartoonist Thomas Nast created the Republican elephant in 1874. The pachyderm was to represent the strength of the Republican vote, but soon became the symbol of the party itself. Nast's drawings of the Republican elephant and his version of the Democratic donkey became lasting images for those parties.

Thomas Nast is remembered for his archetypal American images published during the Civil War and Reconstruction periods. Through his cartoons, he was responsible for transforming Santa Claus from the elf of *The Night Before Christmas* to the modern roly-poly, full-sized gent he is today. Nast also created the image of Uncle Sam, complete with star-spangled wardrobe, top hat, and goatee.

Are the Olympic gold medals actually made of gold?

The difference between winning the silver and the gold medals in the Olympics can be a million dollars in endorsements for the athletes. For the metal smith, however, the difference is about six grams.

According to the Olympic Charter, the first prize in any event "shall be a medal at least 60 millimeters in diameter and three millimeters thick . . . made of silver . . . and gilded with at least six grams of pure gold."

The charter also specifies that the silver medal be made of sterling-quality silver, and the bronze medal be made of genuine bronze. These rules changed, however, for the Albertville Winter Games in 1992. All three medals were made of Lalique crystal plated with gold, silver, or bronze. This was not a cost-cutting measure, since Lalique crystal is more valuable than the metal it replaced.

The Olympic medals are literally irreplaceable—the International Olympic Committee will not replace lost or stolen medals.

Why were the storage facilities at Auschwitz called Canada One and Canada Two?

The Auschwitz concentration camp in Poland was the most notorious of the Nazi era. The names Canada One and Canada Two for the warehouses at the camp came not from the Nazi guards but from their prisoners.

When Europe was thrown into war after the Great Depression, Canada was perceived as a land of peace and plenty. To the prisoners of Auschwitz, Canada represented freedom from their present condition.

But as much as they dreamt about escape, there was as much chance of reaching Canada as there was of reaching the camp warehouses where food, supplies, and confiscated valuables were stored. These warehouses were named after Canada to symbolize the wealth they contained.

If a prisoner was able to sneak successfully into a warehouse and steal food or goods that could be traded for food, it was said he or she had "escaped to Canada."

The irony in this flattering image of Canada lies in its appalling record for accepting refugees during World War Two. Over the course of the war, Canada accepted fewer than 2,000.

Why do chicken and turkey have white and dark meat?

Birds have two types of muscle that appear as white and dark meat when cooked. These muscles are grouped according to their purpose.

White meat comes from muscle fibre used for short bursts of energy. This muscle gets short-term exercise and is used in the fight or flight response.

Dark meat comes from muscle fibre that must work for long periods of time. This muscle fibre contains a special muscle hemoglobin called myoglobin. Myoglobin is similar to blood hemoglobin, but carries more oxygen and less carbon monoxide. The oxygen in myoglobin is necessary for muscles that must work for extended periods.

Since chickens and turkeys are essentially flightless birds, they spend most of their time on their feet. Consequently, the dark meat is found on the drumsticks. Chest and wing muscles aren't used much, so this meat is white.

Flying birds such as ducks and geese use their chest and wing muscles for flight. These muscles contain myoglobin because they require much more oxygen to function properly and therefore produce dark meat.

Why do they put corks in wine bottles?

A sure sign of a cheap bottle of wine is a metal bottle cap. A corked bottle, on the other hand, is more likely to contain a wine that improves with time.

A bottle cap is used on other drinks to stop all chemical reaction. In the case of fine wines, the controlled, continued chemical reactions of the sugars are desired. The cork of a wine bottle allows a small amount of air into the bottle so that this fermentation can continue. This allows the wine to age slowly to perfection. The cork of red wine is longer than that of white wine because the aging process is slower and takes more time.

WHY DO THEY PUT CORKS IN WINE BOTTLES?

Bottles of wine should be stored on their side so that the cork doesn't dry out. If this should happen, too much air may get into the bottle and spoil the wine.

Wine connoisseurs, also known as oenophiles, recommend that you ask your waiter to open your wine in front of you. This is so you can make sure that the bottle has not been opened before or that an expensive bottle has not been filled with cheap wine. There should be no veins in the cork. This is a sign that the wine has turned vinegary.

Comedians have made much of the sniffing of the cork, but this seemingly pretentious ritual does serve a purpose. If the wine has gone bad, the cork will smell musty.

How many balls does a major league team go through in a season?

The number of baseballs a team uses in a season will depend on several variables, including the team's style of play, the budget, and the length of its season, as determined by how it places in the standings. The foul and fly balls caught by fans in the bleachers actually accounts for a very tiny percentage.

The figures here are from the Toronto Blue Jays for 1992, the season the team won its first World Series.

In that championship season, the Jays went through 21,600 balls. The balls cost CN$70 per dozen, for a total cost of $126,000 for the season. This does not include the six thousand balls used in pre-season training.

The majority of balls are used for batting practice. These balls get so "battered" during practice that each one must be replaced every few days. The used balls that still have some life in them are, like an aging player, shipped to the minors.

Why are men and boys called guys?

Guy is a male name that has become generic; that is, any male is a guy, regardless of his given name or age. Informally, use of the word "guy" avoids the problem of what to call a person who is male but of indefinite age. In some cases, to call a female of adolescent age or older a girl is sometimes taken as an insult, yet to call her a woman may sound excessively formal.

"Guy" originates from eastern Europe and the Slavic god Svanto-Vid. This god's followers worshiped him with a frenzied dance. The name was Latinized to Sanctos Vitus, or Saint Vitus, the name given to a Sicilian youth who was martyred, along with his tutor and his nurse in 303 AD. This was at the beginning of a ten-year persecution of Christians instigated by Roman emperors Galerius and Diocletian.

In 16th century Germany, it was believed that one's good health was protected by dancing around a statue of St. Vitus on his feast day. This ritual became a mania and was confused with chorea, a disease of the nervous system causing jerky, involuntary movements. This condition was called St. Vitus's dance, which in France is known as *la danse de Saint Guy*.

Guy took on a very different connotation in 1605 when Guy Fawkes attempted to blow up the British king and Parliament in the Gunpowder Plot. A guy then was an effigy of Guy Fawkes the British carried around and burned in bonfires every November 5th, the anniversary of the conspiracy. Referring to these effigies, a guy was also a person who was considered grotesque.

When this generic use of the name came to America, it soon lost its pejorative sense, since the association with Guy Fawkes had little meaning for the Americans. Instead, guy simply became a slang word for any male.

Guy is also losing its gender-specific meaning. Today, the second-person plural—"you guys"—is used to address mixed groups of males and females, or even groups of females only.

What is the origin of "his name is mud"?

The first person whose name was mud was Dr. Samuel Mudd.

In 1865, John Wilkes Booth assassinated Abraham Lincoln. Booth broke his leg during his escape, but was able to make his way to Dr. Mudd. The doctor, who knew nothing of the assassination, treated the leg and sent the patient on his way.

When Dr. Mudd heard the news the next day, he recognized that the assassin and his patient must be the same person. He reported the incident to the authorities. For his trouble, Dr. Mudd was arrested, tried as a conspirator, and sentenced to life imprisonment.

Since then, a person's name is mud as a result of inappropriate actions.

Dr. Mudd was later pardoned by Lincoln's successor, Andrew Johnson, but not because of this miscarriage of justice. He earned his pardon through his work during an outbreak of yellow fever where he was imprisoned.

In recent years, Dr. Mudd's descendants have campaigned to clear his name. Even though he was pardoned, the conviction remained on the books. The family has argued that Dr. Mudd was unaware of the patient's identity and therefore had no reason not to adhere to the Hippocratic principle of helping someone in need. As recently as June 1992, an application to have the conviction overturned was denied.

How long did it take to build the Trans-Canada Highway?

The idea of a national highway linking all the provinces was a long time in gestation. Records show that public pressure for such a highway was in effect as early as 1910. After the First World War, A. E. Dodd of the Canadian Highway Association fueled the notion when he offered a gold medal to anyone who could drive coast to coast.

In the early 1920s, Dr. Perry Doolittle traveled across the country to promote the cause. As president of the Canadian Automobile Association, Doolittle appealed for support for a national highway.

In 1925, Ford Motors of Canada commissioned photographer Ed Flickenger to drive from Halifax to Vancouver in honour of the company's 21st year. The trip, mostly on dirt roads, took 40 days.

Depression and war redirected public interest, but construction on the Trans-Canada eventually began in the summer of 1950 and was completed in 1970. The 7,821-kilometre highway, stretching from St. John's, Newfoundland to Victoria, British Columbia, is the longest in the world.

The total cost is estimated to be 1.4 billion dollars.

Why doesn't the baking process scorch the paper in a fortune cookie?

The best way to avoid scorching the paper is to keep it out of the oven. Fortune cookie dough is baked flat; once out of the oven the cookie is still soft and is cut to the appropriate shape.

The strip of paper with the message is placed on the soft cookie, which is then folded and folded over again. This process is traditionally done by hand, but in large bakeries machines do the job. Once folded in quarters, the cookie cools off and becomes crispy.

The modern fortune cookie was invented in 1918 at the Hong Kong Noodle Company in Los Angeles by a Chinese immigrant named David Chung. The original messages were quotations from the Bible condensed by a Presbyterian minister.

WHY DOESN'T THE BAKING PROCESS SCORCH THE PAPER IN A FORTUNE COOKIE?

How are television ratings estimated?

In Canada, there are two companies, the Bureau of Broadcast Measurement and Nielsen Marketing Research, that compile information on television programs and their viewers. The Bureau of Broadcast Measurement, also known as BBM, employs a diary method, whereas Nielsen relies on technology.

BBM contacts households at random. People are asked to participate in the survey; those who agree keep a record of their viewing for a one-week period. Every member of the household is given a diary for this record. About 60,000 such diaries are issued nationally during an average ratings period.

Each day is broken down into 15-minute periods between 6:00 a.m. and 2:00 a.m. Participants record the name of the program, the station call letters, and the channel number watched for each quarter hour. They also supply certain background information on themselves.

At the end of the week, participants are to send the completed diaries back to the BBM and the number crunchers interpret the information. About half the diaries are returned.

Nielsen does the same thing for local markets, but uses its famous "people meter" for national surveys. About 1500 televisions across Canada are hooked up to the people meters. The meter records what station and program is being watched; all the members of the Nielsen family have to do is punch in their personal code numbers so the central computer knows who is watching.

At two o'clock every morning, a modem downloads the information to the central computer in Markham, Ontario. Nielsen can then provide information on prime-time programs within 36 hours of broadcast.

Each system has its strengths and weaknesses, but advertisers pay handsomely for the information. They are then willing to spend much greater sums on advertising based on extrapolations of this data.

Why don't dripless candles drip?

There are several types of wax used in the manufacture of candles, each with its own characteristics. Some candles are made from wax that melts and drips down the side. As the liquid wax hardens, it forms the "waxicle" that is part of the traditional candle. This type of candle may be desired for its decorative, traditional look.

In many cases, however, the candle is used for a more practical purpose—to provide light for as long as possible and with as little mess as possible. For this, the dripless candle is preferable. The longest-lasting candles are thick, made of hard wax, and have a thick wick.

The wax used for most dripless candles contains stearic acid. This produces a hard wax with a higher melting point than that of regular wax. Beeswax also has a relatively high melting point. The heat from the wick is insufficient to melt the wax at the outer circumference of the candle. The result is a pool of liquid wax surrounded by a dam of solid wax.

Even a dripless candle will drip, though, if there is a draft. Heat normally rises, but if a draft blows hot air from the wick to one side, the dam of hard wax may melt. Where such a draft is likely, a thicker candle would be better suited.

A thick wick will also prevent dripping, since it is more absorbent than a thin one. Excess liquid wax is absorbed by the wick, which then burns longer. The wax in the wick burns off and there is no build-up.

Why do coaches and managers in baseball wear team uniforms, but not in other sports?

To see the "old" Tommy Lasorda in his team uniform, one might safely conclude that the answer to this question is not found in a greater sartorial sense among baseball coaches and managers.

The baseball uniform was introduced in 1851. The first players to wear uniforms were the Knickerbockers, an amateur team from New York City. Back then, all managers earned their pinstripes the hard way—they wore the uniforms because they were also players on the team. As baseball grew into big business, player-managers became a rare breed, but non-playing managers and other employees of the team continued to wear the uniform as a matter of tradition. Pete Rose of the Cincinnati Reds was a manager-player in 1986.

Two managers bucked the tradition, though. Connie Mack owned and managed the Philadelphia Athletics from the turn of the century to 1950, all the while in civilian clothes. Bert Shotten of the Brooklyn Dodgers also managed his team from 1947 to 1950 without donning the uniform.

Why does biting into aluminum foil hurt teeth with metal fillings?

Biting into aluminum foil can cause a sudden sharp pain if the foil comes into contact with a metal filling in the tooth. This pain is the result of an electric current.

Chemically speaking, most metals have a tendency to give up electrons. When two metals come into contact through an electrolyte, the metal with the greater tendency passes its electrons to the metal with the lesser tendency. This transfer produces an electric current. An electrolyte is any substance that conducts electricity. Battery acid is the electrolyte in most batteries.

When you bite into aluminum foil, your mouth becomes an electric battery. The aluminum foil and the silver in the filling are the posts of the battery, and your saliva is the electrolyte. Biting on the foil completes the circuit. The resulting one to one-and-a-half volts electric current passes through the nerve. This sensation is so painful because, as any victim of a root canal can tell you, the nerve in the tooth is very sensitive to direct contact.

WHY DOES BITING INTO ALUMINUM FOIL HURT TEETH WITH METAL FILLINGS?

How did the band The Barenaked Ladies get their name?

Rock 'n' roll has thrived on its reputation as the rallying cry of rebellious youth. The Barenaked Ladies, from the suburban community of Scarborough, Ontario, fly in the face of this stereotype. The members of the band revel in their middle-class roots. Well after their catapult to success, several members continued to live with their parents.

Mocking the conventions of rock is a characteristic that predates the very existence of The Barenaked Ladies. Their name came from founder Ed Robertson's penchant for making up fake names and histories for fictional rock bands.

Before becoming a Barenaked Lady, Robertson played in a conventional garage band. This band had promised to play a benefit concert for the local food bank's charity drive, but just days before the event, the band broke up. The food bank was depending on the band, so Robertson, not wishing to disappoint the organization, said he had formed another that could play the gig.

When the organizer asked him the name of the band, which did not yet exist, Robertson came up with one of his fictitious names, The Barenaked Ladies, on the spot. Then he recruited his friends to make up a real band in time for the gig.

According to the band's publicity releases, the name is in keeping with the band's point of view. "Barenaked lady" is a phrase a naive eight-year-old might use, and the band is about seeing the world through a child's eyes rather than through the eyes of an adult or even an adolescent.

What are the cockles of one's heart?

The cockles of the heart, as in the expression, "to warm the cockles of your heart," is the deepest, innermost feeling. It comes from the cockle, a mollusk with a shell shaped something like a heart. In fact, the scientific name for the cockle is *cardium*, which comes from the Greek word for heart.

The cockle, like most mollusks, lives most of its life buried in the sand. A cockle within one's heart, then, is a heart buried within a heart. The expression has been around since the 17th century.

Why does one of the characters on *Coronation Street* always wear a Blue Jays jersey?

Coronation Street is the British daytime serial that has been on television since the early 1960s. The program, set in Manchester, has fiercely loyal followings on both sides of the Atlantic.

One of the characters is Jim MacDonald, an ex-soldier turned security guard who is always in a Toronto Blue Jays shirt. Jim MacDonald is played by Charlie Lawson. While the actor was visiting Canada, relatives took him to a Blue Jays game, and he's been a fan ever since. Lawson incorporated the shirt into his role and it is now the character's trademark. According to *The Street*, a fan magazine published by Granada Television, an explanation for the ubiquitous attire has never been worked into the storyline.

Jim MacDonald could wear the Blue Jays logo for many more seasons. After the Blue Jays' World Series victory in 1992, Canadian *Street* fans mailed hundreds of Blue Jay souvenirs to the Granada studios.

What does the name of the Ku Klux Klan mean?

The Ku Klux Klan was formed in 1866 in Pulaski, Tennessee, and has since had several revivals. Some sources say it was originally a social club for six ex-Confederate officers; others say roaming the countryside terrorizing recently freed blacks was its sole intent. In any case, the Ku Klux Klan took its name from the Greek word *kuklos*, meaning band or circle. The club soon degenerated into a violent secret society actively advocating white supremacy. Similar organizations at the time included the Knights of the White Camelia, the White League, and the Invisible Circle.

In 1869, the Grand Wizard of Pulaski disbanded the Klan after it was proven that the Klan was responsible for many acts of violence. Congress passed the Ku Klux Klan Act in 1870 and 1871 in response to continued Klan activities.

A new organization called The Invisible Empire, Knights of the Ku Klux Klan emerged in Georgia in 1915. This new group adopted much of the ritual of the former, and expanded its hate parade to include Catholics and Jews. At its peak in the early 1920s, membership was reputed to be five million, but this declined after the press exposed the Klan's terrorism.

Membership grew again in the 1930s and the 1950s, first in support of fascism, then in opposition to the civil rights movement.

The Klan made minor inroads to Canada in the 1920s. It was first active in Montreal in 1921, but was strongest in Saskatchewan, where its presence was felt during the 1929 provincial election. Several attempts were made in the 1970s to re-establish in Canada, particularly in Alberta and Ontario. However, the American organization disavowed the Canadian Klan when it allowed a black man to join its sheeted ranks.

Why do Detroit hockey fans throw octopi onto the ice?

The octopus is not a creature one normally associates with team sports, but then, there was a time when the same could have been said about the duck.

The tradition of tossing an octopus onto the ice dates back to the 1951–52 season, when the Detroit Redwings were at their peak. The team's standing was in large part the result of goaltending by Terry Sawchuck. The Redwings and Sawchuck beat Toronto in four games straight during the playoffs, advancing them to the semi-finals agains Montreal.

During Game Three against Montreal, a Redwing fan by the name of Peter Cuzimano threw the eight-legged creature onto the ice to encourage the team to stretch the seven-game streak to eight. Finding an octopus wasn't difficult for Cuzimano—he and his brother owned a seafood shop next door to the old Olympia Arena, home of the Redwings.

The gimmick worked—Detroit beat Montreal in four straight. The spell was broken, though, in the next round when Boston knocked the team out of the semifinals four to two.

An octopus is thrown by fans about four times a year, usually during the playoffs. The early octopi were cooked; today they are usually raw. On one occasion, a squid was thrown, causing the ink sacs to break and creating quite a mess.

How do thunderstorms turn milk sour?

The phenomenon of milk souring during a storm is widely regarded as a myth, but there is a scientific basis for this occurrence.

Nitrogen is one of the elements that make up the atmosphere. A lightning bolt will cause the nitrogen around it to combine with oxygen to produce nitrogen oxide, which then reacts with atmospheric hydrogen to produce small amounts of nitric acid.

Before the development of modern techniques, farmers milked cows by hand into an open bucket. This milk was exposed to the open air. If acid is added to milk, the result is curdled milk. If the air contains a small amout of acid as a result of an electrical storm, the normal souring process can be accelerated by this exposure. A bucket of milk that would normally sour in a week would sour in a few days.

HOW DO THUNDERSTORMS TURN MILK SOUR?

Modern dairy practices make milk lightning-proof. Cows are milked by machine, and the milk is kept within a closed system. Milk is pasteurized by heating it to 80 degrees Celsius for 32 seconds to kill all bacteria, then quickly cooled to 3.6 degrees Celsius to avoid a cooked milk taste. Once pasteurized, milk cannot turn sour because it no longer contains the required bacteria, although given enough time it may rot.

Why isn't the border between Saskatchewan and Manitoba a straight line?

In elementary geography class, Saskatchewan is the easiest province to draw—a few straight lines with a ruler and that's it. But the province's eastern border is actually a series of small steps.

Saskatchewan's boundaries were established using an earlier land survey that used Winnipeg as a starting point. The land was mapped out on a grid into square sections, using the lines of longitude to mark the east-west boundaries. The surveyors found that the sections were getting smaller and smaller as they moved north. This is because the lines of longitude are not parallel—they meet at the poles.

To keep the parcels of land uniform and their borders parallel, the surveyors made adjustments to their maps. When the Saskatchewan-Manitoba border was established, these adjustments were incorporated. The corrections were sufficient to keep the sections of land uniform across the province, so its border with Alberta runs straight up the 110th line of longitude. So there's no need to throw out that ruler.

Does the mint still make 50-cent pieces?

The 50-cent piece was the first coin ever issued by the Royal Canadian Mint. It was struck by Lady Grey, wife of the Governor General, in 1870.

The coin is still minted, but it is rarely seen in public today. Banks don't normally keep rolls of the coin on hand because there is so little demand for them. According to the Mint, the 50-cent piece slowly faded away during the 1960s and '70s as we became more dependent on coin-operated machines. Telephones, parking meters, and vending machines are all unable to accept the 50-cent piece, so it is no longer as useful as it once was. (On the other hand, the way vending machines have adapted to the one-dollar coin suggests that this is not the only reason for the decline.)

During the early 1990s, the Royal Canadian Mint issued about a half-million 50-cent pieces annually, down from two million during the mid-1980s. These figures are small compared with those for common coins—in 1987, the mint introduced the new loonie dollar with 205 million coins. Even after the coin entered wide circulation, another 68 million were minted in 1990. Most fifty-cent pieces are uncirculated, and they are immediately snapped up by collectors. Those that enter into general circulation are quickly pulled out again when they end up in the coin jar that everyone has for pennies and unusual coins, such as the 1973 RCMP quarter.

This habit of hoarding coins can have an effect on availability. For example, the mint usually issues between 13 million and 120 million quarters each year, depending on demand. In 1992, about 100 million commemorative quarters were issued in 12 varieties depicting the provinces and territories. Yet these quarters are scarce in pocket change today.

How did the hairstyle called bangs get its name?

The fringe of hair combed forward and cut straight across the forehead gets the name "bangs" from a similar cut on horses. This cut is called a club cut or bangtail, and is commonly part of a show horse's grooming. Bangtail is also a slang term for race horse.

The bang cut was first popular on men and women during the Elizabethan period, and then made a comeback in the 1920s. Bangs are one of the earliest examples of fashion being influenced by the movies. The bang look was popularized by such actresses as Louise Brooks and Anna May Wong. Men, on the other hand, failed to adopt the bang look, as modelled by Moe Howard of the Three Stooges.

The bangs of that period appeared solid. Bangs today are combed and cut so the forehead shows through, giving the style a softer look than the earlier helmet-head.

Why is rubella called German measles?

Rubella is mainly a childhood disease that results in red spots all over the body. The name comes from the Neo-Latin *ruber*, meaning "red," and feminized with *ella*.

While many scientists are immortalized by having their discoveries named after themselves, the one responsible for discovering the cause of rubella had to settle for recognition of his nationality. The virus that causes the disease was identified by German physician Friedrich Hoffmann in 1740.

Rubella is also called French measles, after a French physician named De Bergen. He made further discoveries about the disease in 1752.

Why are detectives called gumshoes?

The sap from rubber trees is called gum. This gum is soft and sticky when hot, and hard and brittle when cold. Consequently, its usefulness prior to the development of vulcanization was limited.

Once this problem was overcome in the mid-1800s, rubber was used in many products. This rubber was still called gum, especially in Britain, even though it was no longer gummy. Among the rubber products were gum erasers, gumboots, and gumshoes.

The heels and soles of gumshoes made little sound compared to hard leather shoes when a person walks in them, so gumshoe became a slang word meaning a sneak or to sneak about.

Gumshoe entered underworld slang around the turn of the century. To the criminal world, a gumshoe guy or gumheel was a policeman. Gumshoe was applied specifically to the detective in *Confessions of a Detective*, published in 1906. By the 1930s, the term was popularized through journalism and the movies.

The term was firmly entrenched in film noir and pulp fiction until it was recently revived in the children's educational program, *Where in the World is Carmen Sandiego*? The globetrotting cast of sleuths on the program features characters called "Gumshoes."

There are other expressions that relate to how one walks. These include slyboots for a cunning person, footpad for thief, and pussyfoot for moving stealthily or timidly. The German *Leisetreter*, or light treader, is a spy, and the French *pied plat*, or flat foot, is a sneaky knave. This is not the same as the American flatfoot, which is applied to police officers who have been on the beat so long the arches of their feet have fallen, resulting in flat feet.

WHY ARE DETECTIVES CALLED GUMSHOES?

Why is skim milk blue?

Milk is a colloidal system, which means it is a liquid with very fine solid particles suspended in it.

Among those solids are milk proteins called caseins. These caseins are used in the production of cheese, plastics and paints. Caseins reflect all the light that hits them, thus they appear white.

Coffee whiteners are made from a similar protein called sodium casein. This casein also reflects all light, so if nothing else, at least it's white.

Milk fat is coated with a layer of caseins. This is where milk products with a high fat content, such as buttermilk and sour cream, get their rich white texture. Skim milk contains less fat, and therefore fewer caseins. Since skim milk has fewer light-reflecting solids, light more easily passes through it. Some of this light is absorbed, and the result is a bluish tinge.

Who invented the hockey puck?

According to the International Hockey Hall of Fame in Kingston, Ontario, the hockey puck wasn't invented. Instead, it evolved even as hockey evolved. Early players probably used lacrosse balls or blocks of wood.

The locker room legend says that, back in the 1880s, a rink manager in Halifax got fed up with broken windows in his facility. To put an end to the damage, he cut the top and bottom off a rubber ball to create something similar to the disk of today. The flat disk stays closer to the ice surface than a bouncing ball or an irregularly-shaped block of wood.

The name for the rubber disk, the puck, comes from *poke* and the German *poken*, meaning to thrust or prod with something narrow.

What is the buck that stops here?

"The buck stops here" is one of several expressions attributed to Harry S. Truman, president of the United States from 1945 to 1952. Truman was known for his pithy comments and his direct approach. Truman had a sign made with this expression, which he kept on his White House desk during his term.

The person who declares that the buck stops here is accepting responsibility, usually with an air of authority and in defiance of obstacles. Although this image fits with the Truman persona, it is unlikely that he was the first to utter this expression.

The buck is the handle of a buckhorn knife. "Passing the buck" is a practice of certain card games where the knife is passed around the table as each player takes his turn as the dealer. As dealer, the player is responsible for keeping the game honest, and making sure that all players pay their stake in the pot.

Why are the upper classes called blue bloods?

The idea that the wealthy have blue blood comes from Spain. People of Spanish descent generally have darker skin than other Europeans. This is because of the Moors from North Africa who invaded the Iberian Peninsula in 711 AD. The dark-skinned Moors bred with the local population, and the result is the darker skin type.

Royalty, however, married only within its own class, without this racial mixing. Skin colour then became a distinction of class. To the darker-skinned common peasantry, white-skinned people, who were generally of the aristocracy, appeared to have blue blood. This was because the blue, oxygen-depleted blood of the veins showed through their skin.

Who are the Joneses that everyone is trying to keep up with?

The expression "keeping up with the Joneses" was originally the title of an early comic strip by Arthur "Pop" Momand. His inspiration for the strip was his own marriage.

Momand and his new bride moved to fashionable Cedarhurst, Long Island, joined a country club, hired a maid, and entertained regularly. Before long, the bills piled up, and it was apparent to the Momands that they were living beyond their means in an effort to keep up with the well-to-do class of Cedarhurst.

Momand and his wife moved to a more modest apartment in New York. They noticed that their situation was not unusual—many of their friends were doing the same, regardless of where they lived. Once financially stable again, Momand was able to see both the humour and the universality of the status trap.

Momand thought the idea that everyone is trying to keep up with someone would make a good comic strip. He prepared six strips and called his feature *Keeping Up With the Smiths*, Smith being the most common name in North America. He changed the name to Jones, feeling that *Keeping Up With the Joneses* had a better sound.

He submitted his strip to the McClure newspaper syndicate, and was told that it would take a week to consider. The strip was accepted in three days, and was launched in February 1913. *Keeping Up With the Joneses* ran for 28 years, appearing in hundreds of newspapers at its peak of popularity. The strip was adapted into short-subject film comedies and a stage musical, and was collected and published in book form in 1920, making it one of the first comic books.

Why do prayers end with "Amen"?

The word "Amen" comes from *aman*, the Hebrew word meaning "to confirm." In Hebrew ritual, Amen is used to emphasize acceptance of the Covenant. In the New Testament, many statements by Christ begin with Amen to emphasize their truth. In some versions this is translated to "verily."

Closing a prayer with "Amen" is the religious equivalent of "10-4" or "So long for now." In the Christian church, it is the means by which the believer validates what has been said and then concludes communication with God. Validation and confirmation is also what we mean when we say, "Amen to that, brother!"

Why is brown wrapping paper called kraft paper?

Kraft paper is the brown utility paper associated with the rolls of wrapping paper used at the old general store or by butchers for their meats. Brown cardboard boxes are also made from kraft paper.

Kraft paper is made from a special type of pulp also called kraft. Sodium sulfide and sodium hydroxide are mixed in with the pulp at a high temperature to dissolve the lignin, the material that holds the wood together. The result is pulp with long brown fibres of cellulose. This pulp is the strongest available to paper manufacturers.

This process was developed in Danzig, Germany in 1879. Six years later, the first kraft paper was produced for commercial use at a mill in Sweden.

Kraft takes its name from the German word *kraft*, meaning "strength."

How are ostrich feathers harvested?

Ostrich feathers for commercial use are produced by smaller birds that are specially cross-bred for this purpose. Ostriches grown for meat and leather do not produce feathers of sufficient quality.

Ostriches ranched for their feathers produce about 90 plumes every seven months. The best plumes are about 18 inches long and are found under the wings and on the tail. When the time comes to harvest the

HOW ARE OSTRICH FEATHERS HARVESTED?

feathers, each bird is herded into a V-shaped barrier and held in place from behind by a rubber strap. The birds do not struggle; instead they just stand still.

The living feathers have blood in them and the shaft is dark. Dead feathers contain no blood and the shaft is white. Left on their own, these dead feathers would eventually drop out. Before this can happen, the rancher cuts the feather about an inch from the body. Two weeks later, the remaining stub is plucked so that a new feather can grow.

One batch of feathers from one bird will bring in about $100, although during the heyday of ostrich feather fashion, the same feathers would be worth about $60,000 in today's money. The largest market for ostrich feathers today is Japan, where they are used to brush down automobiles before painting. Ostrich feathers are also used in Silicon Valley to clean computer chips.

What makes Canadian bacon Canadian?

Canadian bacon is an American term for back bacon that comes from the loin eye of the hog. The loin eye is the large muscle that runs up both sides of the backbone. When cut in cross section, it looks like an eye, hence the name.

In Canada and Britain, the whole loin eye and belly are cured to make bacon. Once cured, this meat is cut into back and side bacon. In the United States, only the belly is cured. This becomes side bacon. Consequently, Canadian back bacon sold in the United States is named after its home country.

Back bacon is much less fatty than side bacon. Well-butchered back bacon can be up to 90 percent lean, whereas Canadian side bacon is 40 to 45 percent lean. American side bacon is even fattier, with only about 30 percent lean meat.

Why is "no." the abbreviation for number?

Like many other abbreviations that don't seem to make sense, such as "lb." for pound and symbols of many chemical elements, "no." is translinguistic.

The abbreviation was first known to be used in 1583. At that time, many elements of Latin lingered in European languages. Often the abbreviation for a word came from its Latin origins. Such is the case for number, which in Latin is *numero*.

Originally "no." meant "numbering" or "which number," as in this quote from 1661: "They goe two months, & then bring forth a blind off-spring like bitches, no. eight or nine." Today, the abbreviation is used to identify a single item by its designated number, as in "Love Potion No. Nine."

Incidentally, the modern abbreviation for pound comes from its Latin word, *libra*.

What time is it on the Peace Tower on the five-dollar bill?

The picture on the front of the five-dollar bill is of the original Centre Block building on Parliament Hill. This building was destroyed by fire in 1916. The engraving is based on a photograph taken sometime during Sir Wilfred Laurier's term as Prime Minister; Laurier is also on the front of the bill.

The photograph was retrieved from government archives when the bill was redesigned in 1986. The exact date of the photograph is unknown, and even the year can be estimated only to within a 15-year period.

The time shown on the tower clock is 10:10, although this may not have been the actual time when the photographer tripped the shutter. The hands of the clock may have been deliberately moved to that time specifically for the photograph. Ten minutes after 10 is usually the time on pictures of clocks and watches because of the visual balance when the hour and minute hands are in that position.

What is the origin of the Olympic symbol?

The modern Olympic Games were first played in 1896, but the five-ringed symbol did not make its appearance until two decades later.

The Olympic Games were re-established through the efforts of Pierre de Coubertin of France. Coubertin also designed the emblem for the flag, in 1913. On a white field, there are five interlocking rings, each of a different colour: blue, yellow, black, green, and red. Coubertin's intention was to make the emblem as international as possible. Every country in the world at that time had at least one of the six colours (including the white of the background) in the emblem.

The five rings represent the five parts of the world: Europe, Asia, Africa, Australia, and, together, the Americas.

The host city is obligated to fly the Olympic flag wherever other flags are flown, to affirm the international status of the city during the time of the Games. The emblem was first used on a flag at the 1920 Games held in Antwerp, Belgium.

Where did the golfer's "bogie" come from?

The bogie has been a part of golf since the 1890s. Today, a bogie is one stroke over par, but at that time, a bogie *was* par.

The word comes from "bogie man," that same demon used to frighten children into behaving. "The Bogey Man" was also in vogue at the time because of a music hall song with the lines, "Hush, hush, hush, here comes the Bogey Man . . . He'll catch you if he can."

While playing a round at the Great Yarmouth course in Norfolk, England in either 1890 or 1891, a Major Charles Wellman found it difficult to beat the standard score—similar to what we call par today. Major Wellman claimed that the standard score of the course was "a regular Bogey Man." Dr. Thomas Browne, secretary of the Great Yarmouth club, then adopted Bogey as the name for the fictional player who played every hole in the standard score.

Dr. Browne, who was in the Royal Navy, introduced his imaginary player to the United Services Club at Alverstoke in Hampshire, where many of the members were army and navy officers. One player, Captain Vidal of the Royal Engineers, claimed that such a player must be an officer, so the rank of Colonel was conferred on Bogey.

The standard score of a course is the score a competent player should be able to achieve if no mistakes are made. Later, the standards of the game were raised, but the bogey score remained the same. The result is that a bogey score is now one stroke over par.

Colonel Bogey of the golf links is the same Colonel Bogey of *The Bridge on the River Kwai*. The inspiration for *The Colonel Bogey March* came to Major F. J. Ricketts after a jaunt across a fairway in 1913. At first, Ricketts, who didn't play golf, ignored a golfer's warning of "fore!" Exasperated, the golfer whistled to get Ricketts' attention. The two notes of the golfer's whistle stayed with Ricketts, and that night he wrote *The Colonel Bogey March*, with the whistle as the opening notes.

The Colonel Bogey March is best-known today from the 1957 film, *The Bridge on the River Kwai*, starring Alec Guinness. It was the tune whistled by the British prisoners to keep up their spirits as they built the bridge for the Japanese.

Who came up with "do, re, mi"?

Identifying notes of the musical scale by syllables rather than letters is called solmization. The Chinese and Greeks had such a system, and Indian music has long used a syllable tone system.

Solmization, which takes its name from *sol* and *mi*, is a part of solfege, or solfeggio, a series of vocal exercises used to teach students to recognize notes and to improve vocal technique. It is similar to vocalises, which are vocal exercises where the notes are sung to a vowel.

Modern solmization was developed by Guido d'Arezzo sometime in the 11th century. He introduced the syllables *ut re mi fa sol la* for the notes C to A. These are called the Guidonian syllables. The system remained unchanged until the 16th century, when the French introduced *si* to complete the octave, and *ut*, which is not easily sung, was replaced by *do*.

Other systems were introduced between the 17th and 18th centuries, but these did not last. Some of these syllable combinations included *bo ce di ga lo ma ni* and *la be ce de me fe ge*.

The best-known use of solmization is in *The Sound of Music*, where Julie Andrews gives fanciful definitions to each of the syllables, beginning with "*Do*, a deer, a female deer."

What is the origin of "putting on the dog"?

To put on the dog is to behave in a bumptious or pretentious manner, or to appear self-important. The expression is believed to date back to the 1860s, where it was used by the students of Yale University.

Lyman H. Young defined the expression in his book, *Four Years at Yale*, published in 1871, this way: "To put on the dog is to make a flashy display, to cut a swell."

At that time, Blenheim and King Charles cocker spaniels were very popular among the wealthy. To the students of Yale, these dogs were the height of snootiness.

What is the origin of the hung jury?

A jury's verdict could lead to a hanged defendant, but a hung jury could save his life. A hung jury is one in which its members are unable to reach agreement over the defendant's guilt or innocence.

The term comes from the American legal system, and dates back to the 19th century. It has nothing to do with the noose; instead, it refers to "undecided," which is a definition of hung that is now obsolete. For example, in his published correspondence, Benjamin Franklin wrote to a friend that he was "hung" about a particularly troubling issue.

The defendant whose case leads to a hung jury isn't off the hook yet. If a decision cannot be reached, the case is retried with a new jury. If that jury is also hung, the case is tried and retried until either a decision is reached or the prosecution drops the charges. The greatest number of times a case has been tried in Canada is four.

WHAT IS THE ORIGIN OF "PUTTING ON THE DOG"?

Who invented the jigsaw puzzle?

Puzzles similar to the jigsaw variety made of baked tile have been found among the ruins of ancient Egypt. The modern jigsaw puzzle, however, dates back to 1762. That's when English printer John Spilsbury saw an opportunity to capitalize on the boom in children's educational publishing. Spilsbury printed maps, mounted them onto hardwood, cut them into pieces, and sold the resulting puzzles as educational tools.

The map puzzles were so successful that other printers issued similar puzzles of their own. Maps continued to dominate the market until the 1780s, when poems and quotes from the Bible printed on newspaper-sized sheets of paper were mounted on wood and cut into puzzles. Illustrations were not commonly used until the introduction of color lithography in the early 1800s. Puzzles of this era were hand-made of fine hardwoods and were therefore very expensive, costing as much as a labourer could earn in a week.

The puzzle craze took off in the United States in the 1860s, when Milton Bradley and the McLaughlan Brothers introduced mass production and modern marketing techniques. These companies produced their puzzles on less-expensive soft woods, and increased production by cutting the printed designs several layers thick at a time.

The jigsaw puzzle was so-named after the Philadelphia Centennial exhibition in 1876. It was here that the power scroll saw, later called the jigsaw, was introduced. The blade of this saw is very thin, allowing the curved cuts that were ideal for cutting interlocking pieces. Prior to the scroll saw, puzzle pieces did not interlock, except occasionally along the outside pieces.

The name "jigsaw puzzle" became obsolete in the 1890s, when the cutting table and die press were developed. With the die press, which cuts the cardboard to pieces with one impression, Parker Brothers entered the jigsaw puzzle market in 1909. This company's puzzles were noted for their special pieces shaped like snowflakes, stars, flowers, and so on.

The modern jigsaw puzzle emerged by 1920 with the development of steel ribbon dies. The steel of this die is so thin and flexible that the designer can bend sharp curves to create the characteristic tongue and groove of each piece. The challenge to the designer is to shape each piece so that no two are alike. These dies could cut the cardboard images into 500 or more pieces, thereby creating a whole new market for jigsaw puzzles among adults.

Jigsaw puzzles of this era were so cheap to produce, they were often given away as advertising premiums. Characters from radio, film, and newspaper comics were licensed to puzzle manufacturers in the 1930s; many of these cheaply-produced puzzles command high prices among puzzle collectors today.

The deluxe jigsaw puzzle on hardwood remained a favourite of the upper classes. Parlours that rented puzzles and created custom puzzles for these tastes emerged in the 1930s. One of the most famous was Par Puzzles, established by Frank Ware and John Henriques of New York. Both were victims of the Depression in 1931 when they realized that most people complete a given puzzle only once before putting it away. They saw a market in renting puzzles to customers instead. Soon they opened their own parlour, with a glamourous clientele of puzzle enthusiasts that included Bing Crosby, Gary Cooper, Stephen Sondheim, and Marilyn Monroe.

Special clients warranted special puzzles. Every puzzle custom made for the Duke of Windsor had pieces cut in the shape of his four cairn dogs. Puzzles for the Duchess were made with pieces cut in the shape of her maiden initials, WW, in her own handwriting.

The Par Puzzles emporium was also visited regularly by British agents during World War II, who were suspicious of Nazi agents rumoured to have traded in secret messages left in hollowed-out puzzle pieces.

Par's puzzles were noted for their originality and difficulty. Each puzzle came in a black box with no picture and a deliberately misleading title. The challenge was to complete the puzzle in Par time, which was the time it took for Ware and Henriques to complete the puzzle. The name Par Puzzles still exists, and a few puzzles are still produced by the company, but the puzzle parlour closed its doors in the early 1970s.

How are hummingbirds able to hover?

The 300 species of hummingbirds are the most accomplished of all flying animals. They are able to fly straight up, down, forward, and backward—they can even fly sideways.

Hummingbirds feed mainly on flower nectar. To do so, they must maintain a stationary position so they can draw the nectar up their long bills. This and other feats of flying are possible because the hummingbird's shoulder joint, where the wing is connected to the body, allows far greater movement than on other birds. Thus, the hummingbird can beat its wings for upward lift, then shift the angle of its wings and beat for forward movement, then balance that with a beat for backward movement. In other words, the hummingbird floats near the flower by "treading air."

The hummingbird beats its wings up to 70 times per second. To do this, the hummingbird must burn energy ten times faster than a human does when running. This very high metabolic rate and resulting heat loss means that the hummingbird must feed every 15 to 20 minutes on its high-energy diet of plant sap and flower nectar. Hummingbirds also feed on insects and spiders for protein.

Most hummingbirds are found in tropical and semi-tropical climates, but some also migrate as far north as Alaska. These migrating birds, as well as those in cooler mountainous regions, are able to conserve energy by regulating their body temperature at night. By reaching a state similar to hibernation, they are able to lower their normal temperature of 40 degrees Celsius to 24 degrees.

When was the horse domesticated?

Horses have been part of human culture for at least 10,000 years. Most of that time, however, the horse was not a mount or a co-worker, but a source of food. From cave paintings in Spain and archaeological sites in North America, we know that wild horses, much smaller than those of today, were hunted. Scientists believe over-hunting to be the likely cause of extinction for the North American horse.

It was probably in Central Asia around 3000 BC that horses were first domesticated rather than hunted for food. Horses of this time were too small for humans to ride; donkeys were the preferred means of transportation. After the development of the wheel, horses, which are much swifter than donkeys, were enlisted to pull chariots for the Mesopotamian army. This was a major development in the history of warfare, since troops were now mobile.

Soldiers did not start riding horses until 900 BC. This was made possible by selective breeding of horses for size, and by the invention of the bit. With the bit and reins, the soldier was better able to control his mount while using his weapons.

Chariot racing was a staple of the Olympic Games in Greece since their inception, but it was not until the XXXIII Olympiad in 624 BC that the first mounted horse race was recorded.

How many calories are there on the gum of a postage stamp?

Many types of glue and gum have a starch base. This starch contains a few calories. But Canadian postage stamps are low-cal, since they are coated with a rubber-based gum. This gum contains no calories.

Canada Post doesn't know the actual formula for the glue on postage stamps. The glue base is PVA, or poly-vinyl alcohol, which is water-soluble. The three companies that supply pre-glued paper to Canada Post closely guard their secret glue recipes, but the companies must certify that the paper meets Health and Welfare Canada standards.

Once printed, the sheets of stamps must be certified again that they meet Health and Welfare standards.

Why is yawning contagious?

During the middle ages, people thought that yawning was brought on by the Devil. The uncontrollable urge to yawn gave him an opportunity to enter the soul. If the first attempt failed, he might trigger another yawn and try again, or he might move on to the next person in the room. The standard defense against such an attack was the sign of the cross.

Until recently, scientists thought that yawning was a way of expelling a build-up of carbon dioxide and taking in a lungful of fresh air. That's why we yawn when we are tired or bored, when breathing is shallow, or when we are in a stuffy room. This theory was unsupported by experiment, however. When test subjects were placed in an oxygen-rich room, they yawned just as much as ever.

The prevailing theory is that yawning in humans is an evolutionary hold-over that has very little to do with how tired we are. This theory says that yawning is a defense mechanism—a way of saying "back off."

Yawning is common among primates; in fact, the male leader of a troop of chimpanzees will yawn about four times as much as other males. By yawning—and baring his teeth—the leader is able to protect his territory and intimidate the others into falling into line.

We humans usually yawn when we are bored or tired. According to the defense theory, when we yawn out of boredom, we are really saying, "I'm getting out of here!" The polite person, of course, stifles the yawn and suffers in silence.

When we yawn out of sleepiness, we are attempting to mark our territory, telling others to stay away. This is seen as a defense against the vulnerability we feel as we fall asleep, but is not caused directly by sleepiness.

Yawning is highly contagious, but not because of anything in the air. The counter-yawn seems to be a psychological response. The reacting yawn can be triggered by seeing another person yawning. The old yawn-as-a-breath-of-fresh-air theory was also shot down by the fact that the first yawner need not be in the same room—a televised yawn will trigger yawns among viewers, even when the program is interesting.

The counter-yawn can also be triggered by just thinking about yawns. This very page is likely setting off a few yawns (no snide remarks, please—*ed*.).

According to the defense theory, this yawn is an automatic response to the implied threat of the first person's yawn. For example, among the chimpanzees, the individual who yawns back at the leader is the one most likely to stand up to the leader's authority. The individual who yawns least is the most submissive. A counter-yawn is a way of saying, "Oh, yeah? You and whose army?"

In the end, however, scientists have been unable to prove conclusively any theories about yawning, so they remain just theories.

How do chameleons change colour?

The top layer of a chameleon's skin cells are transparent. Underneath are four layers of coloured cells. The cells in the top coloured layer are red and yellow. The next two layers are blue and white. Underneath is a layer of dark cells called melanophores.

The chameleon will change its colours for many reasons, such as temperature, a change in the lizard's mood, or the need for camouflage. The colours of the chameleon can change within seconds because the coloured cells in the skin expand and contract. For example, when the cells of the yellow layer contract, the blue layer shows through the spaces between them. The result is blue or green, depending on the degree of contraction. With its red, yellow, and blue cells, the chameleon can

HOW DO CHAMELEONS CHANGE COLOUR?

produce any colour. Intensity is controlled by the white and melanophore cells.

The melanophore layer shows through when all other cells contract. This layer is most useful when the chameleon wishes to blend in with tree bark.

How do bees make honey?

Winnie the Pooh was so addicted to honey it clouded his judgment and ruled his life. If he knew how it was produced, he would probably find it less tempting.

Honey is produced by worker bees, the females that are destined not to reproduce. Instead, they live to nurse the queen's larvae, build the cells of the hive, and gather food before dying of exhaustion. The worker lives for about six weeks, compared with the queen's three- to five-year life span.

When a worker bee travels from flower to flower, she gathers nectar at the flower's base. This nectar is a liquid secreted by the plant, and has a high sugar content. The bee sucks up the nectar with her long tongue, and the nectar is then stored in the honey stomach. This honey sac is past the gullet and is part of the abdomen, next to the stomach used to digest the bee's own food.

The bee's body produces enzymes that digest the nectar, breaking it down to the simpler sugars dextrose and levulose. When the bee returns to the hive, she regurgitates the partially-digested nectar. As moisture evaporates and the mixture thickens, more enzymes are added. The result is a highly-concentrated source of energy that is fed by the workers to the larvae, queen, and male drones.

The flavour of honey depends on the type of flower visited by the bees. Most commercially-produced honey comes from clover. To produce one pound of honey, 550 bees must collect nectar from 2.5 million flowers.

Why does aluminum foil have a dull and a shiny side?

Aluminum foil is made two sheets at a time. The two layers are pressed between two rollers, much like a newspaper as it rolls off the press. Because the surface of these rollers are smooth, the outer side of each aluminum sheet, when pressed through the rollers, are polished by these rollers. This is the shiny side. The two sides of the aluminum that face each other remain unpolished and appear dull.

Common wisdom says it is important which side is which when preparing food. Since the shiny side is reflective, it is thought that food should be wrapped with the shiny side inside for cooking, and on the outside for freezing. Many professional home economists argue that, once the foil is crumpled, it doesn't matter which side is which.

Why did Columbus sail on behalf of Spain instead of Italy?

Christopher Columbus was an Italian from Genoa, but his plan to sail westward to Asia was beyond the means of the divided republics and kingdoms that made up the Italian peninsula. Financing would have to come from an empire.

Columbus first approached King John II of Portugal for money to pay for ships and crew. John turned down the plan, saying that it was too expensive. That was just a ruse, as the king's spies gathered details of the planned excursion. He sent his own ship on the journey, which traveled as far as the Cape Verde Islands before heading back due to stormy weather.

Columbus then went to Spain, where the plan reached Mendoza, Archbishop of Toledo. With the archbishop's help, Columbus made his pitch to King Ferdinand and Queen Isabella. The matter was referred to a council of scholars, which turned it down.

Columbus dispatched his brother Bartholomew to England to seek the aid of Henry VII. Pirates sympathetic to England and hostile to Spain captured Bartholomew, and he did not complete his journey until several years later. In the meantime, an appeal to the court of France was also rejected. Finally, because of the rivalry between Spain and Portugal, Isabella agreed to sponsor the endeavour after hearing of John II's interest in western expansion.

With three ships and a crew of about 90, Columbus sailed from Spain for Japan. The journey began on August 3rd, 1492. Land was sighted on October 12. This landing is believed to be in the Bahamas; the crew also made landings at the islands of Hispaniola (Haiti and the Dominican Republic) and Cuba, which Columbus believed to be Japan and China. He continued to believe for the rest of his life that he had found the western route to Asia.

In March 1493, Columbus returned to Spain a hero and was made Admiral of the Seas and Viceroy of the New Lands, as per his agreement with Isabella. He probably should have rested on his laurels. Still in search of Marco Polo's mythical Quinsay, the City of Gold, he set sail again six months later, this time reaching Puerto Rico and Jamaica. To make up for the lack of expected gold, Columbus took to the slave trade on the side. Meanwhile, trouble was brewing in Hispaniola, where he had earlier established a Spanish colony. The result was charges of mismanagement, and on his third voyage was ordered back to Spain in chains.

Though his titles were revoked, he was permitted a fourth voyage in 1502, during which he explored the coast of Central and South America. He was marooned on Jamaica for over a year before a ship came to return him to Spain. In 1506, Christopher Columbus died in poverty while the initial investment paid windfall dividends to the Spanish empire, especially after the discovery of Aztec gold only a few years later.

What causes a fever to break?

Normal body temperature, as taken from an oral thermometer, is 37 degrees Celsius. This temperature may vary by two degrees either way, however, since body temperature varies from person to person. An individual's normal temperature also varies over a 24-hour period. Any abnormal increase in body temperature is called a fever.

Any factor that affects the body's heat-regulating mechanism can bring on a fever, including hot weather, strenuous activity, and dehydration. However, fever is most commonly a symptom of bacterial or viral infection. In this case, the fever is caused by toxins, the poisonous chemicals released by this bacterial or viral activity.

As toxins build up, body temperature rises. The patient may become delirious, or go into convulsions or a coma. The toxins then build up to the point where they begin to destroy the infecting organisms that produced them. When this occurs, the fever "breaks," and the body temperature begins to return to normal.

Why are Washington, Jefferson, Lincoln, and Roosevelt the presidents on Mount Rushmore?

South Dakota's famous monument to past presidents was first planned by sculptor John Gutzon de la Mothe Borglum and state historian Doane Robinson. The theme was to be the Louisiana Purchase, the American acquisition of 828,000 square miles from France for 15 million dollars. The territory, between the Mississippi River and the Rocky Mountains, more than doubled the area of the United States. The idea for the theme was prompted by the recent discovery of a tablet buried by French explorer Pierre de La Verendrye in 1743.

The sculpture took 14 years to reach its present state of completion. After Borglum's death, his son Lincoln took over the project until funds ran dry in 1941. Some of the details are unfinished, and there are no plans to complete the sculpture as originally designed.

According to a report published in 1941 by the Mount Rushmore National Memorial Commission, Borglum expanded the theme to include several stages of American expansion—each president was a key figure at different stages in that expansion. George Washington led the rebel army in the War of Independence and was first president of the new republic. Thomas Jefferson was president at the time of the Louisiana Purchase in 1803. Theodore Roosevelt led the famous charge up the San Juan Hill during the Spanish American War of 1898; the US gained possession of the Philippines and Puerto Rico as a result of that war.

And, according to the report, Abraham Lincoln was president when the United States purchased Alaska from

WHY ARE WASHINGTON, JEFFERSON, LINCOLN, AND ROOSEVELT THE PRESIDENTS ON MOUNT RUSHMORE?

Russia. Lincoln, however, was assassinated in 1865, and the Alaska purchase was in 1867.

Updated National Parks Service publications on Mount Rushmore explains the selection of presidents differently. It says, "These four figures represent the birth and trials of the first 150 years of the United States. Individually they represent the ideals of the Nation. George Washington signifies the struggle for independence and the birth of the Republic, Thomas Jefferson the idea of representative government, Abraham Lincoln the permanent union of the States and equality for all citizens, and Theodore Roosevelt the twentieth century role of the United States in world affairs."

Both versions carry equal authority. The first is based on interviews with Borglum's wife, the second comes from a book written by his son. The real story remains unknown—the elder Borglum never stated his reasons for his choice of presidents.

And that,

Dave Petursson, Doreen Smith, Bill Bolstadt, Brian Dickie, Margaritte Bonay, Kelly Nelson, Carmelle Moyer, Beverly Mah, Ivo Fodar, Gene Reiger, Kathy Hyska, Tony Sebastian, Doris Merkosky, Stu Robertson, Armstrong Mettle, Don Keindel, Phillip Highland, Brynn Choquette, Peyson Rock, Chris Shannon, Jim Legin, Nettie Lozinsky, Linda Morgan, Judy Adamson, Randy Reeves, Anna Malawski, Ian Christie, Brad Cuttington, Pat Connelly, Arnold Smith, Bree Buck, Neil Holt, David Angell, Joshua Good, Gordon Martin, Mark Vukas, Shelley Sharkey, David Nadeau, Elizabeth Nemeth, Neil Norgaard, Carol-Ann Larose, Todd Larochelle, Jane Martin, Des Holden, Jane Thompson, David Ross, Heidi Gruetzner, Jamie Morton, Barbara McNeil, Betty Schmidt, Alan Not, Linda Navalaowski, Steve Ouhet, Selfrid Norberg, Scott Lauchan, David Stoft, Marshall Drummond, Kathy Phillips, and Lindsay Roberts,

is the answer to your Good Question!

Index

If you liked this book, you may want to order the original

That's a Good Question!

How did the TV show "The Fifth Estate" get its name? And what are the other four estates?

What is the oily film on apples from the supermarket?

Why do Bic pens have a hole in the side while other pens don't?

Why are Nova Scotians called "bluenosers"?

Why do men's and women's clothing button on different sides?

Why do most clocks with Roman numerals on the face show the number four as IIII instead of the standard IV?

Are dolphins working for the US Navy?

What were the results of the artificial iceberg experiments of World War II?

What is the origin of the word "ketchup"?

Why is the popcorn at the movies fluffier than home-popped popcorn?

Why are the keys on a typewriter arranged the way they are?

Copies of **That's a Good Question!** are available from the publisher. To order, please complete the order form on the back page.

You may also want to order the #1
Canadian National Bestseller

That's a Good Question, Canada!

Where does the blood come from for operations by
veterinarians?

What is the origin of the 1960s civil rights theme song *We
Shall Overcome*?

How much paper can be obtained from the average-sized
tree?

How do seedless fruit trees reproduce?

Who invented popcorn?

How does a spider get its first line across?

Why is there no channel one on TV sets?

What makes the rattle in a rattlesnake's tail?

Why do they make screws with different kinds of heads?

Who is the Murphy of Murphy's law?

Why do birds face the same direction when perched on a
high-tension wire?

Copies of **That's a Good Question, Canada!** are available from the publisher. To order, please complete the
order form on the back page.

And the third book in the series,

What the Heck Is a Grape Nut?

answers these tantalizing questions

Why is there a crescent moon on outhouse doors?

How did bureaucratic delay become known as "red tape"?

Why is the boxing ring called a ring when it's square?

Where did the 1960s peace symbol come from?

Why are bulldozers yellow?

What was the first television commercial?

Why don't the Governor-General and his wife have to pay GST?

Who is the man on Canadian Tire money?

Where does the expression "the whole nine yards" come from?

What's a blue moon, and how often does one happen?

What were Canada geese called before Confederation?

Copies of **What the Heck Is a Grape Nut?** are available from the publisher. To order, please complete the order form on the back page.

And why not the fourth book,

Why Do Golfers Yell Fore?

Have any of these questions ever crossed your mind?

What tribe was Tonto from?

Why are chalkboard erasers striped?

How did the poop deck get its name?

Why did 45 rpm records have big holes in them?

Why does Alaska have a panhandle?

Where does the line, "It was a dark and stormy night," come from?

Why is there a "#" on touch-tone telephones?

How does the electoral college in the United States work?

What does mistletoe have to do with Christmas?

Why do we clink glasses during a toast?

Why do turnips taste better if they're harvested after the first frost?

Why do zebras have stripes?

Copies of **Why Do Golfers Yell Fore?** are available from the publisher. To order, please complete the order form on the back page.

Please print clearly; this will be your mailing label.

Name _____

Address _____

_____

_____

I'd like

_____ copies of the original That's A Good Question!
ISBN 0-9694287-0-7

_____ copies of That's A Good Question, Canada!
ISBN 0-9694287-2-3

_____ copies of What The Heck Is A Grape Nut?
ISBN 0-9694287-6-6

_____ copies of Why Do Golfers Yell Fore?
ISBN 0-9694287-7-4

_____ copies of Who On Earth Is Dr. Pepper?
ISBN 1-896015-00-X

_____ total copies x $11.00 each = $_____ .
(Price includes postage, handling, and GST)

Once completed, mail this form to
Script: the writers' group
Suite 200, 839 - 5th Avenue S.W.
Calgary, Alberta, Canada
T2P 3C8

Please allow two to three weeks for delivery

Also available from Script

It's How You Play the Game:
The Inside Story of the Calgary Olympics
(ISBN 0-9694287-5-8)

by Frank W. King, chief organizer of the 1988 Winter Olympics

A gripping, entertaining, and emotional account of the best-ever Olympic Games. This 376-page hardcover book is beautifully illustrated with 32 pages of colour photographs. The book is dedicated to the 12,310 Games-time volunteers, all of whom are named in the book. To order your copy now, complete the order form (or a photocopy) and mail it along with a cheque or money order for $29.95 for each book ordered.

Hawrelak: The Story
(ISBN 0-9694287-8-2)

by Diane King Stuemer

A biography of controversial Edmonton mayor Bill Hawrelak. Hawrelak was twice forced from the mayor's chair under the cloud of political scandal, only to be swept back each time by a landslide. One of the most colourful and memorable political figures in western Canada's history, he left an indelible mark on the city of Edmonton. To order your copy now, complete the order form (or a photocopy) and mail it along with a cheque or money order for $19.95 for each book ordered.

Taking Control of Your Blood Pressure:
Steps to a Healthier Lifestyle
ISBN 0-9694287-4-X

by Lorna Milkovich, Beverly Whitmore & Peter Henderson, Ph.D.

A workbook written for people with high blood pressure.

You can:
- assess your own lifestyle.
- learn how your lifestyle affects your blood pressure.
- learn how to control weight, eat a balanced diet, manage stress, quit smoking, and exercise safely.
- learn how blood pressure medication works.

Written by health professionals working in a hypertension clinic. Start taking an active role in your treatment today. To order your copy now, complete the order form (or a photocopy) and mail it along with a cheque or money order for $16.00 for each book ordered.

(All prices include handling, postage, and GST.)

I would like to order _____ copy (copies) of *Hawrelak: The Story* (ISBN 0-9694287-8-2) at $19.95 for each copy of the book ordered (includes handling, postage, and GST).

I would like to order _____ copy (copies) of *It's How You Play the Game: The Inside Story of the Calgary Olympics* (ISBN 0-9694287-5-8) at $29.95 for each copy of the book ordered (includes handling, postage, and GST).

I would like to order _____ copy (copies) of *Taking Control of Your Blood Pressure: Steps to a Healthier Lifestyle* (ISBN 0-9694287-4-X) at $16.00 for each copy of the book ordered (includes handling, postage, and GST).

I have enclosed a cheque or money order for _____ copy (copies) for a total of $_____.

Please print clearly; this will be your mailing label.

Name: _____

Address: _____

City, Province: _____

Postal Code: _____

Clip this form and mail it to:

Script: the writers' group

Suite 200, 839 - 5 Avenue S.W.

Calgary, Alberta T2P 3C8

Please allow two to three weeks for delivery.

GST Registration # 124167594